Local Planning
in Scotland

In memoriam
Keith Ferguson, MA, LLB, DPA,
lawyer, writer and father,
who excelled in all three professions.

Local Planning Reviews in Scotland

Andrew C Ferguson

Solicitor and Notary Public

John Watchman

Solicitor and Notary Public

Avizandum Publishing Ltd
Edinburgh
2015

Published by
Avizandum Publishing Ltd
25 Candlemaker Row
Edinburgh EH1 2QG

First published 2015

ISBN 978-1-904968-07-8

British Library Cataloguing in Publication Data
A catalogue record for this book is available from the British Library

Typeset by AFS Image Setters Ltd, Glasgow
Printed and bound by Martins the Printers, Berwick-upon-Tweed

Contents

3   Local Planning Reviews: Governance and General Approach to Decision-making   71

4   Preparing and Submitting a Notice of Review and Period for its Determination   93

5   Local Review Body Pre-meeting Process   106

Preface

For those of us who plough the criss-crossing furrows of town and country planning on a daily basis, it is easy to forget just what an alien landscape it presents to most lay people. Concepts such as the development plan, material considerations, environmental impact assessments, residential amenity, traffic management, design, and massing, are easy to explain in principle, but not necessarily so easy to grasp for someone who might only be involved in a planning application once or twice in a lifetime.

Such involvement will often be in relation to that person's own house, or a neighbour's, where money has been scraped together for a much dreamed-of kitchen extension, or a new build on a piece of land adjacent to the existing property. It might even be something as basic as replacing windows in a historic block of flats.

Any of these types of development will, since 2009, almost certainly now be dealt with by a planning official of the local authority under delegated powers. The property owner – with or without a professional adviser, such as an architect – will view that alien landscape for the first time, and be given to understand that a decision will be forthcoming in due course. In the case of replacement windows, it may just be the window installer that deals with such technicalities as planning permission. For a neighbour wishing to object, it is likely to be the start of a lone journey across the landscape.

Statistically, it is far more likely that the property owner will get the permission they ask for – and their neighbour will find, if they did not know before, that there are no third party rights of appeal in Scottish planning law. However, the planning application could be refused. It could be granted subject to conditions the property owner had not expected, and does not find acceptable. There could be a delay at the planning department which the owner finds unacceptable, and which her architect tells her is technically beyond the time in which a decision should have been granted.

In any of these situations, the owner's remedy – as in the first two cases a decision notice will inform her – is to ask for a review by a local review body. At this point the property owner, her neighbour, and even her architect, surveyor or other professional adviser will likely find themselves in new territory altogether, strangers in a strange land. This book is intended to help them find their way.

At the other end of the spectrum of delegated decisions, property professionals planning a 49-house development, or commercial or industrial proposals of a similar scale, will also have the option of making an application for review in the event of an unsatisfactory decision, or one which is outwith the prescribed timescales. The chapters that follow are also intended for them. Although the local review body system has been in place for five years now, it is still relatively new, and subtly different in its operation among the thirty-three planning authorities. Even seasoned professionals may have limited experience of them.

Finally, the text is aimed at those in local authorities who have the task of administering, advising, or otherwise assisting with the running of a local review body. With the current demographics of most council departments, and the ongoing shrinkage in staffing budgets, there is little doubt that there will be continuing turnover in local authority expertise in this area.

Any law book has to set out the policy reasoning and intellectual concepts behind both the legislation, and any case law which interprets it; at the same time, many readers will simply be looking for a 'how to' guide through the *terra incognita*. We have tried to strike a balance between these two aims, with the early chapters explaining the genesis of the local review body system, and the later chapters leading the reader step by step through the process.

No book is created in a vacuum, and we would like to thank the following people in particular for their assistance: Michelle McDermott, for typing Andrew's half of the manuscript; Greg

Lloyd, June Barrie and Steven Paterson for reading and commenting on the next-to-final drafts; and last but not least Margaret Cherry, our editor and publisher, for her patience and professionalism. The idea for this book was first discussed with her over lunch, and further developed over coffee in the Royal Museum of Scotland: a far more civilised approach than most publishing ventures, these days.

We have endeavoured to state the law as at 1 May 2015. The opinions expressed on the law are not intended to bind those of our employers.

Andrew C Ferguson
John Watchman
May 2015

Tables of legislation

STATUTES

ORDERS, RULES AND REGULATIONS

EU MATERIALS

Table of cases

Introduction

No piece of legislation is created in a vacuum. Rather, it has its own unique context and it captures a moment in time: a crystallisation of the, then, collective will of the legislators of the day to try to make change for the better. However, that is not to say that such collective will as exists cannot contain apparently contradictory aims.

The Planning etc (Scotland) Act 2006 ('the 2006 Act') was an attempt to improve the efficiency of the planning system in Scotland to allow investment to grow the economy, create jobs and opportunities and to ensure that local people were better able to participate in decisions that affect them. At the same time it was to ensure that no developments would go ahead where community voices had not been fairly heard. Further, it sought to restore confidence and trust in the planning system, and revitalise it as a critical tool for shaping the future of the communities in Scotland's cities, towns and countryside.

In particular, the package of reforms was prepared with a view to subduing the clamour for a third party (also know as a community) right of appeal against the grant of planning permission. One element of the reforms was taking away an applicant's right to submit a planning permission appeal to the Scottish Ministers, and replacing it in the case of 'local development' planning permission applications where the decision at first instance was one that could be taken by a planning authority officer with the right to require a review by the relevant planning authority 'local review bodies' (committees of local authorities and the Loch Lomond and The Trossachs National Park Authority).

Local planning reviews in Scotland came into operation in 2009. Chapter 1 of this book considers the road to reform and addresses matters including the still unresolved issue of compatibility with rights set out in the European Convention on Human Rights as well as offering some comments about outcomes of the development management reforms. More than five years on from its introduction, the system of local planning reviews in Scotland has still something of an experimental quality to it, and the following chapters outline particular areas that require close attention by all those involved in the local planning reviews system including applicants for review and their agents, those clerking and advising a local review body, members of local review bodies and others (such as statutory consultees and those who have made objections to a proposed development that may or will be subject to consideration by a local review body).

Before 2009, planning authorities were allowed to decide which planning decisions were taken by a committee and which by officers. In another innovation, which is intertwined with the operation of local review bodies, the Town and Country Planning (Scotland) Act 1997 ('the 1997 Act') as amended by the 2006 Act and related regulations sets down minimum requirements for a scheme of delegation, requiring authorities to delegate a great majority of decisions relating to local planning applications to officers. This is discussed at Chapter 2.

Chapter 3 explores the basic governance requirements of a local review body. Being a committee of the planning authority, there is a suite of relevant legislation which needs to be considered and applied by those administering it. The planning authority's standing orders will also come into play, as well as other procedural aspects, which will need to be followed to avoid any possibility of challenge on grounds of inept procedure. The issue of whether the local review body is undertaking a re-hearing of the case presented to the original planning officer or a *de novo* examination of the application itself is also examined here.

Chapter 4 deals with the making of an application for review itself. It considers the statutory forms, and offers advice and assistance in completing them. The question of what additional information to include, as well as what new information can legitimately be presented at that stage, is explored. The interaction between the provisions of the 1997 Act as amended by the 2006 Act and the relevant related regulations needs careful interpretation, by applicants and planning authority staff alike. Finally, the chapter addresses other aspects of the regulations concerning the application, such as the requirement for copies of documents.

Chapter 5 sets out the pre-meeting arrangements in relation to a local review body, a crucial stage at which several matters need to be undertaken by the planning authority correctly. One such aspect is the completion of any statutory requirements (such as notification) which have not, so far, been dealt with in relation to the original planning application. Those who have made representations at the planning application stage must be notified and given the opportunity to make further representations which, in turn, applicants will then have to have an opportunity to comment on.

The papers are then to be assembled for the first meeting, a process which may involve some key decisions about what papers are legitimate, whether duplication is allowed or is, indeed, necessary, and whether some form of report, pulling the papers together, can be allowed or is helpful.

Chapter 6 then discusses the crucial first meeting of the review body, which can frequently be the determinative meeting. The role of planning and legal advisers, as well as the crucial role of the Chair of the local review body, is examined. The role of the Chair is unusually onerous in relation to this and other meetings of the local review body, particularly given the limited role which planning and legal advisers ought to have in the context of a review of an officer decision. It is fair to say that it is not a role which even experienced committee Chairs were used to prior to 2009, and the necessity of proper reasons for the review body's decision being discussed openly and lucidly at the meeting is explored fully.

Similarly, the need for initial procedural decisions, as to whether the review body has enough material to decide the case, may require close attention by the Chair. Should there not be sufficient material, there are key points to then decide on how the local review body wants to obtain additional information.

This gathering of further information is then considered in Chapter 7. The legislation provides for an initial procedural meeting although, in practice, that may well be dispensed with if decisions and further procedure have been taken at the first meeting. The local review body can obtain the further information it needs for a decision by written submissions, by site inspection, or by way of a hearing, as well as a mixture of the three. Again, procedural accuracy is important so that all parties – review body members, advisers, applicants, and those who have made representations – are clear what is required of them at subsequent meetings.

Chapter 8 deals with making and recording the decision. As the local review body is formally a committee, there is a requirement for a minute of the meeting to be produced. However, the legislation has set down that there should be a decision notice and good practice requirements for such a notice as well as timeframes for issue of the notice are discussed.

Finally, in Chapter 9, the difficult issue of what further avenues for redress lie open to an applicant are set out. These include the prescribed route of statutory application to the Court of Session and avenues such as complaints to a council's 'Monitoring Officer', Royal Town Planning Institute ('RTPI') complaints, complaints to the Standards Commission or Scottish Public Services Ombudsman complaints are dealt with, as well as the possible grounds for making an application to the Court of Session for judicial review of a decision taken by a local review body.

Chapter 1

Local Planning Reviews in Scotland

The Scottish Government is responsible for overseeing the effective functioning of land-use planning in Scotland. The primary responsibility for operating that planning system rests with the 32 local authorities and the two national park authorities in Scotland.

The most recent legislative package of land-use planning reforms was introduced by the Planning etc (Scotland) Act 2006 and related secondary legislation. Those reforms mainly came into operation in 2009.

This chapter includes comments about the road to reform and coming into force of the legislative provisions (the 'hierarchy of developments', 'local development' schemes of delegation, and the establishment of 'local review bodies' and related review provisions) which underpin local planning reviews in Scotland. It also refers to related law and guidance.

Those readers looking to access details regarding the relevant legislation about local planning reviews in Scotland (other than details about the 'hierarchy of developments' and those developments which are 'local developments', which are covered in this chapter) and the related law and guidance which underpin local planning reviews should turn immediately to the chapters which follow.

Change of policy regarding planning, particularly planning appeals

The planning reforms of the noughties were conceived as a package of measures that would subdue the clamour for third parties to be given the right of appeal (sometimes referred to as a 'community right of appeal') against the grant of planning permission.[1]

The rhetoric was about increasing local powers and enhancing local democratic accountability. For instance it was said by the, then, Minister for Communities (Malcolm Chisholm MSP) in his introduction in the Scottish Executive's 2005 White Paper *Modernising the Planning System*[2] that the proposed reform of the planning system 'gives powers back to planning authorities and gives them the freedom to organise the delivery of a better local service with local decisions and local accountability'.

It is not clear what powers the proposed planning reforms identified for repatriation. The reforms were also apparently introduced with the aim of reducing the planning permission appeals workload of the Scottish Ministers' reporters as much as with the aim of increasing local democratic accountability and, at the same time, centralising power in the Scottish Executive to have the final say on development plans.

Since 7 March 1994 development plans have become the primary document for determining whether a proposed development will be allowed. The determination of an application for planning permission, unless material considerations indicate otherwise, must be made in accordance with the development plan.

Prior to the most recent reforms coming into operation members of planning authorities took the final decision on local plans. Now, in effect, the current planning regime provides for the Scottish Ministers' reporters to take the final decision on local development plans. These decisions are almost invariably taken following an examination by correspondence as development plan hearings are rarely convened. A local development plan authority has very limited grounds for departing from the recommendations set out in an examination report prepared by a person appointed by the Scottish Ministers. In effect, the stated grounds should not

---

1 The Royal Commission on Environmental Pollution in its 23rd report *Environmental Planning* (2002) recommended that third parties should have a right of appeal against decisions on planning applications in certain circumstances.

2 www.gov.scot/Publications/2005/06/27113519/35231

come into play if the work undertaken by the reporter has been carried out properly.[3]

The obvious potential for a significant centralisation of plan making was subsequently reduced by the Scottish Government. Its February 2009 Circular 1/2009: *Development Planning* was prepared without the benefit of public consultation.[4] That circular refers to proposed local development plans being the planning authority's 'settled view' as to what the final content of the plan should be. This was allied with a light touch examination process that eschewed an examination of the soundness of the plan, and required an examination of the 'appropriateness and sufficiency' of the content of a proposed plan. These provisions signalled that the transfer of power to the Scottish Ministers' reporters might not be as great as originally thought. The current Scottish Government Circular 6/2013: *Development Planning* continues with the earlier approach and places greater emphasis on the local planning authority's 'settled view' of plan content. It restates that the reporter is not 'tasked with making the plan as good as it can be' and underlines that any intervention by a reporter should only take place where the proposed plan is 'clearly inappropriate or insufficient'.

Experience following the introduction of local planning reviews in Scotland indicates that, every year, between 500 and 600 cases are now being considered by local review bodies – thus enhancing local democratic accountability – as opposed to the Scottish Government (through its Directorate for Planning and Environmental Appeals ('DPEA')).

The transfer of powers to planning authorities was much more modest than envisaged at the time the Planning etc (Scotland) Bill was being considered by the Communities Committee of the Scottish Parliament. At that time, it was envisaged that the Scottish Ministers' powers would be significantly restricted in planning permission appeals. The Scottish Ministers and the DPEA would only

---

3 See the Town and Country Planning (Grounds for Declining to Follow Recommendations) (Scotland) Regulations 2009 (SSI 2009/53).
4 This can be contrasted with, for example, the Scottish Government issuing a consultation paper in December 2008 about its proposed revision of Circular 12/1996: *Planning Agreements.*

have an appellate jurisdiction where, for instance, the proposed development was for 300 or more dwellings. The provisions ultimately enacted reduced that threshold to 50 or more dwellings.

Overview of 'local development' planning reviews

It has been said that the introduction of local planning reviews in Scotland sought to reduce the number of planning permission appeals made to the Scottish Ministers, to increase local accountability and to ensure that resources were used effectively and proportionately.[5]

In general the current legislative regime for 'local development' planning applications can be summarised as one which:

- removed an applicant's right of appeal to the Scottish Ministers against an adverse decision taken by the planning authority's appointed officer on any application for a 'local development' planning permission, or consent, agreement or approval required by a condition imposed on such a permission or the failure of the planning authority's appointed officer to determine the relevant application within the prescribed period or any extended period agreed in writing between the applicant and that officer;

- established planning authorities in Scotland (as opposed to the Scottish Ministers or the person appointed by them (known as a 'reporter')) as the final judges of the planning merits of applications for 'local development' planning permission or consent, agreement or approval required by a condition imposed on such a permission which were not determined in the first instance by a committee of a planning authority; and

- retained the Court of Session as the final judge of the lawfulness of a planning authority's actions or omissions as a result of the court determining either a statutory application under section 239 of the Town and Country Planning (Scotland) Act 1997 ('the 1997 Act') or a petition for judicial review – although one might have expected that the desire for local

---

5 Audit Scotland, *Modernising the Planning System* (2011) at para 53.

decision-making might have resulted in jurisdiction in, at least, challenges by way of statutory application to local review body decisions being transferred to local sheriff courts. (The Licensing (Scotland) Act 2005 and the Civic Government (Scotland) Act 1982 provide precedents for related statutory applications to the sheriff court.)

The Scottish Government's aims were to:

- encourage a more proportionate approach in determining applications for planning permission with proposed developments being assessed and determined according to their scale and complexity;
- focus the resources of bodies such as the Scottish Environment Protection Agency and Scottish Natural Heritage on the relatively small number of proposals for any 'national development' or any 'major development' so that the planning applications could be project managed (for instance by the use of an administrative tool known as a 'processing agreement') and handled efficiently; and
- promote applications for 'local developments' being assessed and determined at a local level by the relevant planning authority – the local authority or the Loch Lomond and The Trossachs National Park Authority as the case may be – primarily by planning authority officers; which, in turn, would decrease the workload of both planning authority committees and the DPEA and free up capacity for the efficient processing of matters including those matters within the DPEA's remit such as the examination of development plans and the determination of the more substantial or controversial planning permission appeals.

The 'innovative statutory structure'[6] of local planning reviews in

---

6 *Carroll v Scottish Borders Council* [2014] CSOH 6 para 53.
7 Planning etc (Scotland) Act 2006 (Commencement No 7) Order 2009 (SSI 2009/100) and Planning etc (Scotland) Act 2006 (Commencement No 9) Order 2009 (SSI 2009/219).

Scotland came into operation on 3 August 2009.[7] In summary, the relevant legislation including the 1997 Act makes provision for:

- a hierarchy of developments for development management purposes – any planning permission application for proposed development is allocated to one of the three classes of development (applications for a 'national development', a 'major development' or a 'local development');

- a requirement for planning authorities to prepare and adopt, and keep under review, a statutory scheme of delegation made under the 1997 Act for applications for planning permission for a 'local development', or for consent, agreement or approval required by a condition imposed on a 'local development' planning permission;

- an applicant's right to require a review by the planning authority (through its 'local review body') of decisions taken by an officer appointed under such a scheme of delegation (including a deemed refusal of a 'local development' application) – instead of an applicant having a right of appeal to the Scottish Ministers; and

- prohibiting the introduction of any matter (ie topic) at a review by the planning authority unless (a) the matter not being raised was a consequence of exceptional circumstances; (b) it is a new matter which could not have been raised before the appointed officer's decision; or (c) the matter relates to the development plan or a 'material consideration' (ie a relevant planning issue); the prohibition does not exclude further evidence about an existing matter.[8]

Devolution and town and country planning in Scotland

8 Town and Country Planning (Scotland) Act 1997 ('1997 Act'), ss 26A, 43A and 43B; Town and Country Planning (Hierarchy of Developments) (Scotland) Regulations 2009 (SSI 2009/51), Public Services Reform (Planning) (Local Review Procedure) (Scotland) Order 2013 (SSI 2013/24) and Town and Country Planning (Schemes of Delegation and Local Review Procedure) (Scotland) Regulations 2013 (SSI 2013/157) (the '2013 Regulations').

The Scottish Parliament was established in July 1999. The Scottish Parliament and the Scottish Ministers have no power in relation to reserved matters and cannot make legislation or take (or fail to take) action that is incompatible with any of the 'Convention rights' or with 'Community law'.[9] The obligation to act compatibly with 'Convention rights' also applies to public authorities.[10]

So, for instance, a petition for judicial review may be submitted to the Court of Session challenging the legality of legislation of the Scottish Parliament on the basis that the legislation is not compatible with rights guaranteed by the European Convention on Human Rights.[11]

Town and country planning is not one of the matters reserved to the UK Government under the Scotland Act 1998.

However, even before the establishment of the Scottish Parliament, the Scottish Office in January 1999 published its consultation paper *Land Use Planning under a Scottish Parliament*. This signalled that land-use planning in Scotland was one area ripe for reform following the establishment of the Scottish Parliament.[12]

Post-devolution consultation about planning reform

After the Scottish Parliament was established extensive public consultation was undertaken about the reform of the law of town and country planning in Scotland. From 2001 the Scottish Executive issued a suite of consultation papers about the reform of the land-use planning system in Scotland.

One of those consultation papers was the 1 April 2004 paper *Rights of Appeal in Planning*.[13] The focus of that paper was whether to widen rights of appeal in planning by the introduction of a 'third-party right of appeal' (sometimes referred to as a 'com-

---

9 Scotland Act 1998 (see ss 29, 30, 53 and 57(2) and 126(9) and Sch 5) and Human Rights Act 1998 (see ss 1, 6 and 8 and Sch 1).

10 Human Rights Act 1998 (see s 6 and Sch 1) and Scotland Act 2012.

11 See, eg, Lord Hope of Craighead 'Judicial review of the Acts of the Scottish Parliament', SCOLAG Journal August 1999, p 107.

12 See, eg, (1999) 71 SPEL 6 and (1999) 72 SPEL 26.

13 www.gov.scot/Publications/2004/04/19206/35624

munity right of appeal'). That paper did not consider the transfer of power from the Scottish Ministers (and their appointed reporters) to planning authorities to decide whether to uphold certain planning application decisions taken in the first instance by planning authority officers.

2005 White Paper *Modernising the Planning System*

A government White Paper sets out detail of future government policies on a particular issue. Publication of a White Paper allows government the opportunity to gather feedback before presenting its policies as a Bill.

Despite the significant amount of consultation by the Scottish Executive from 2001, many of the fundamental elements of the current planning regime in Scotland were first announced by the Scottish Executive's White Paper *Modernising the Planning System*, which was published in June 2005 ('the 2005 White Paper').[14]

The proposals in the 2005 White Paper were conceived with the aim of delivering commitments to 'improve the planning system to strengthen the involvement of local communities, speed up decisions, reflect local views better and allow quicker investment decisions.' It identified the challenge as 'establishing a planning system that works for Scotland, introducing the changes necessary to provide a quicker, more transparent and more effective service and to create a system better suited to operating in the context of a Scottish Parliament and a single tier of local government.'

The 2005 White Paper included the first announcement by the Scottish Executive of its proposals to:

- introduce a hierarchy of developments to enable application for different types of development to be dealt with in different ways;
- require planning authorities to make schemes of delegation under the 1997 Act for 'local development' planning applications; and
- empower planning authorities to determine (through their local review bodies) an applicant's requirement for review

14 www.gov.scot/Publications/2005/06/27113519/35231

where the decision at first instance was taken by an officer appointed by virtue of a 'local development' scheme of delegation made under the 1997 Act.

Those proposals signalled government's intention to transfer some 'local development' application powers (and the related work) away from the Scottish Ministers (and the DPEA) to planning authorities.

In December 2005 the Scottish Executive published both a digest of responses[15] and an analysis of responses[16] to the 2005 White Paper.

The digest of responses records representations made by a wide spectrum of Scottish society (local authorities, non-departmental public bodies, the development industry, the business community, professionals and professional bodies, community councils, voluntary organisations and individuals). The responses to the 2005 White Paper relevant to the establishment of local planning reviews in Scotland are considered below.

Planning etc (Scotland) Bill and Planning etc (Scotland) Act 2006

The Planning etc (Scotland) Bill ('the Bill') was introduced in the Scottish Parliament on 19 December 2005[17] along with the relevant Policy Memorandum[18] and Explanatory Notes.[19]

The proposals in the Bill included the insertion into the 1997 Act of new provisions including section 26A (Hierarchy of developments); section 43A (Local developments: schemes of delegation) and section 43B (Matters which may be raised in a review under

15 www.gov.scot/Publications/2005/12/2084221/42223
16 www.gov.scot/Publications/2005/12/0195339/53401
17 www.scottish.parliament.uk/S2Bills/Planning%20etc.%20(Scotland)%20-Bill/b51s2-introd.pdf
18 www.scottish.parliament.uk/S2Bills/Planning%20etc.%20(Scotland)%20-Bill/b51s2-introd-pm.pdf
19 www.scottish.parliament.uk/S2Bills/Planning%20etc.%20(Scotland)%20-Bill/b51s2-introd-en.pdf

section 43A(8)).

The Bill provided a framework for legislative reform. However, the Scottish Executive's proposed planning regime was substantially based on the details which were to be provided in secondary legislation. Many expressed concerns about the level of detail that would become apparent only with the introduction of secondary legislation.

The Scottish Parliament's Communities Committee ('the Committee') considered and reported on oral and written evidence regarding the Bill, including the Scottish Executive's proposals for a hierarchy of developments, requiring planning authorities to make schemes of delegation under the 1997 Act and establishing local planning reviews.[20]

The 10 May 2006 report of the Committee recorded that the Committee considered that this absence of detail restricted its ability to scrutinise certain provisions contained in the Bill.

No drafts of any secondary legislation were published for consultation by the time the Bill was passed by the Scottish Parliament on 16 November 2006, let alone in time for the Scottish Parliament's consideration of that Bill. The Bill for the Planning etc (Scotland) Act 2006 received Royal Assent on 20 December 2006.

The relevant secondary legislation about schemes of delegation and local reviews and the hierarchy of developments was made in 2008 and 2009 respectively and came into force in April and August 2009.

Hierarchy of developments

The Scottish Executive proposed to make the planning system more fit for purpose by measures including introducing a hierarchy of developments into the planning system, to enable effective planning for a range of different types of development, and to respond appropriately to planning applications according to the size and impact of the proposed development.

---

20 www.scottish.parliament.uk/S2CommunitiesCommittee/Reports/cor06-05-vol01.pdf   and   archive.scottish.parliament.uk/business/committees/communities/reports-06/cor06-05-Vol02-00.htm

The Scottish Executive's proposal to introduce a hierarchy of developments was not the first time that such a proposal had been made.

Dobry Report 1975

In 1973 George Dobry QC was appointed to consider the development control (including the planning permission appeals) system then in place. In general, his approach was to retain the system of planning permission applications and planning permission appeals but to streamline the management of that system. In his 1975 *Review of the Development Control System*[21] he recommended:

- dividing applications for planning permission and planning permission appeals into two categories:
  - ○ 'Class A' comprising: all simple cases; all applications conforming with an approved development plan; development which only just exceeds that permitted by the General Development Order (even when not allocated for that use in the development plan) and the approval of reserved matters related to applications for planning permission classed as 'A' when outline planning permission was sought; and
  - ○ 'Class B' comprising all other planning applications;
- that applicants for planning permission should retain the right of appeal against any adverse local authority decision to the Secretary of State; and
- there should be a simpler appeals procedure for 'Class A' applications.

However Dobry's recommendations were rejected. The UK Government subsequently encouraged planning authorities to identify for priority handling applications for planning permission which in their judgment would contribute most to national and local economic activity.

2005 White Paper: hierarchy of developments for handling
21 HMSO, ISBN 0-11-750896-9.

planning applications

The 2005 White Paper proposals for a hierarchy of developments for the purposes of development management envisaged four categories of development:

- national development;
- major development;
- local development; and
- minor development (development with permitted development rights).

The 2005 White Paper indicated that 'national developments' would be identified in the National Planning Framework. It also indicated that 'minor development' was defined by the scope of permitted development rights. The 2005 White Paper also signalled a review, and anticipated extension, of those rights and, in turn, removing many 'minor' developments from the scope of the planning system and, consequently, the requirement to make planning applications.

However, the 2005 White Paper did not identify the descriptions of 'major development' and their related thresholds or criteria. This, in turn, meant that there was no clarity about the scope of a 'local development'.

The 2005 White Paper stated that:

> 'The vast majority of the 50,000 plus planning applications decided annually are for small-scale changes to commercial or industrial buildings and work by householders to alter their properties. These developments are local in nature, and do not have an impact on the wider area. Decisions on these planning applications should, therefore, be taken at the local level.'

The proposals for a hierarchy of developments for handling planning applications was said to be 'a means to securing better outcomes from the planning process'.

The analysis of responses to the 2005 White Paper noted widespread support for the principle of a hierarchy of developments, but a clear view that there was a need to get the detailed definition of each of the categories right.[22]

Planning etc (Scotland) Bill

The Policy Memorandum for the Bill stated, at paragraphs 91–93, that:

- the policy intention is that the Scottish Ministers will be able to designate different types of development as coming within a particular category of the hierarchical framework, in secondary legislation;
- applications for proposed developments identified as falling within one of the designated categories (national, major and local) will during the development management process be subject to different procedures for submission, processing and determination depending on the category in which they fall;
- the aim of this proposal was 'to allow for a more proportionate approach by focusing engagement and scrutiny on the more complex development management issues, while at the same time seeking to streamline and speed up those processes where possible'; and
- public bodies will be able to better prioritise the way in which they use resources more effectively; facilitate national political debates about infrastructure; devolve local decision making; involve local people more effectively and encourage development that is sustainable.

Scottish Parliament's consideration of the hierarchy of developments

The 10 May 2006 report of the Scottish Parliament's Communities Committee recorded its support for the introduction of the hierarchy of developments as a means of ensuring that resources are appropriately directed to where they are most needed in terms of processing applications for development, and the Committee's

22 www.gov.scot/Publications/2005/12/0195339/53452

view that the categorisation of developments under the hierarchy by regulations was an area of key importance.[23]

Provisions about the hierarchy of developments for handling planning applications

Indications about the likely content of the relevant secondary legislation were given by the Scottish Executive to the Scottish Parliament about development descriptions, thresholds and criteria for 'major developments' and, in turn, 'local developments' before the Bill was passed. Those indications suggested that there would be a substantial transfer of power from the Scottish Ministers on appeal to planning authorities (through their local review bodies). For instance, a development of up to 299 homes would be a 'local development' and, in turn, would fall within the jurisdiction of the planning authorities.[24] Ultimately the transfer of power to planning authorities was much more modest: for instance, the Scottish Ministers retain jurisdiction for planning appeals where the planning application is for at least 50 homes or the housing site area is at least 2 hectares – so, for example, a development of 30 homes on a 3-hectare site would be a 'major development' which ultimately could be the subject of an appeal to the Scottish Ministers.[25]

In November 2007 a public consultation was carried out on draft regulations for the planning hierarchy.[26] The consultation comments received[27] led to a number of changes from the original

---

23 www.scottish.parliament.uk/S2CommunitiesCommittee/Reports/cor06-05-vol01.pdf

24 Michaela Sullivan, Deputy Chief Planner, Communities Committee, Official Report, 11 January 2006, column 2774–5. See also letter dated 23 March 2006 from Malcolm Chisholm MSP, the then Minister for Communities, to the Communities Committee of the Scottish Parliament, published as one of the papers for the 28 March 2006 meeting of that committee.

25 Town and Country Planning (Hierarchy of Developments) (Scotland) Regulations 2009 (SSI 2009/51).

26 www.gov.scot/Publications/2007/12/11104120/0

27 www.gov.scot/Publications/2008/06/02094814/0 and see also the analysis of responses at www.gov.scot/Publications/2008/12/02144950/0.

proposals. For instance, the threshold for the number of homes was reduced by half (from the proposed 100 to 50).

The Town and Country Planning (Hierarchy of Developments) (Scotland) Regulations 2009 ('the 2009 Regulations'), which came into force on 6 April 2009 and which are still in force, provide details about the hierarchy of developments.[28] The hierarchy of developments for handling planning applications relates to planning applications for:

- 'national developments': those developments or classes of developments designated as such in the National Planning Framework under section 3A(4)(b) of the 1997 Act;
- 'major developments': those classes of developments belonging to the categories of development described in the 2009 Regulations (see below); and
- 'local developments': those developments other than 'national developments' and 'major developments'.

Major developments

The descriptions of 'major developments' are:

1. *Schedule 1 EIA Development*: development of a description mentioned in Schedule 1 to the Environmental Impact Assessment (Scotland) Regulations 1999[29] (other than exempt development within the meaning of those Regulations).

2. *Housing*: construction of buildings, structures or erections for use as residential accommodation where either (a) the development comprises 50 or more dwellings, or (b) the area of the site is or exceeds 2 hectares.

3. *Business and General Industry, Storage and Distribution*: construction of a building, structure or other erection for use (a) as an office; (b) for research and development of products or processes; (c) for any industrial process; or (d) for use for storage or as a distribution centre where either (i) the gross floor space of the building, structure or other erection constructed as a result of the development

---

28 SSI 2009/51.
29 SSI 1999/1.

exceeds 10,000 square metres; or (ii) the area of the site is or exceeds 2 hectares.

4. *Electricity Generation*: construction of an electricity generating station where the capacity of the generating station is or exceeds 20 megawatts.

5. *Waste Management Facilities*: construction of facilities for use for the purpose of waste management or disposal where the capacity of the facility is or exceeds 25,000 tonnes per annum – for facilities for sludge treatment use, a capacity to treat more than 50 tonnes (wet weight) per day of residual sludge.

6. *Transport and Infrastructure Projects*: construction of new or replacement roads, railways, tramways, waterways, aqueducts or pipelines where the length of the road, railway, tramway, waterway, aqueduct or pipeline exceeds eight kilometres.

7. *Fish Farming*: the placing or assembly of equipment for the purpose of fish farming within the meaning of section 26(6) of the 1997 Act where the surface area of water covered is or exceeds 2 hectares.

8. *Minerals*: extraction of minerals where the area of the site is or exceeds 2 hectares.

9. *Other Development*: any development not falling wholly within any single class of development described in paragraphs 1 to 8 above where either (a) the gross floor space of any building, structure or erection constructed as a result of such development is or exceeds 5,000 square metres; or (b) the area of the site is or exceeds 2 hectares. Typically this category involves mixed use developments or developments for uses such as retail, school, nursing home, hotel or a law court not falling wholly within the specified description of development.

The 2009 Regulations also address the issue of extensions to developments. Regulation 2(1)(b) of the 2009 Regulations in effect provides that any change to or extension of a development (whether to an existing major or local development) is only to be treated as major where such a change or extension alone would meet or exceed the relevant appropriate threshold or criteria. So, for instance, neither a proposed 3,000 square metres extension to an existing 2,000 square metres office or to an existing 5,000 square metres office would be a 'major development' because, although the total floorspace meets or exceeds the 5,000 square metres threshold, the proposed extension is not in itself at least 5,000 square metres.

The current Scottish Government guidance, and a more detailed narrative, about the 2009 Regulations, is set out in its Circular 5/2009: *Hierarchy of Developments.*[30]

'Local developments': schemes of delegation and local review bodies

Prior to 3 August 2009 the vast majority of planning applications were determined by planning authority officers under powers given to them by schemes of delegation made under the Local Government (Scotland) Act 1973 which provides that local authority decisions can be taken by the (full) council, a committee (including a sub-committee) of the council or a council officer.[31] Authorisation to take any specific action, decision etc is contained within a scheme of delegation.

Before 3 August 2009 any challenge to any adverse planning application decision or the failure to take a decision within the prescribed or agreed extended period was addressed to the Secretary of State (and post-devolution to the Scottish Ministers and then the Scottish Government via the Scottish Executive Inquiry Reporters Unit and then the DPEA respectively). In the main, planning permission appeals were decided by a person appointed by the Secretary of State and, post-devolution, by the Scottish Ministers. That person is known as a 'reporter'.

The development management regime aimed to increase the number of planning applications determined by planning authority officers using their delegated powers and to transfer powers to local authorities to review 'local development' decisions taken by those officers, thereby freeing up resources in both planning authorities and the DPEA which could be

---

30 www.gov.scot/Publications/2009/07/03153122/0
31 Local Government (Scotland) Act 1973, s 56. See Chapter 2.

focused on handling and determining planning applications for 'major developments' more efficiently.

Planning permission appeals

The right to submit any planning permission appeal to central government was a cornerstone of government policy and modern planning law in the United Kingdom.

Post-June 1948

In general the current planning system is still substantially based on the foundations laid by the UK planning Acts of 1947.[32] That is true in particular about determining applications for planning permission against the background of policy set out in development plans. From 1 July 1948 that legislation replaced landowners' development rights with the rights:

- to make an application for planning permission to a planning authority;
- to have any such application determined in accordance with the law and having regard to planning policy; and
- for an appeal to central government by the applicant for planning permission against any adverse planning authority decision and for the Secretary of State to deal with the application for planning permission as if the application had been made to the Minister in the first instance.

1988 review of administrative law in the United Kingdom

In the 1988 Report of the Committee of the JUSTICE-All Souls Review of Administrative Law in the United Kingdom *Administrative Justice: Some Necessary Reforms*[33] the Committee considered the suggestion that ordinary planning appeals should be decided by the structure plan authority rather than by, or on behalf of, the

---

32 Town and Country Planning Act 1947 and Town and Country Planning (Scotland) Act 1947.
33 Clarendon Press, 1988, ch 10.

Secretary of State. The report states that:

> 'What underlies this suggestion is the constitutional objection that, under the present system, the decision of the elected members who comprise the local planning authority may be overturned by [the person appointed by the Secretary of State] – who may be a civil servant. Hence we have been urged to recommend that the [person appointed by the Secretary of State] should submit a report, not as previously to the Secretary of State (and as [that person] does in about 5 per cent of cases), but to the . . . planning authority with responsibility for the structure plan. We prefer the present system. The [person appointed by the Secretary of State] is an impartial adjudicator and the Secretary of State is sufficiently distanced from local political pressures.'[34]

2004 local authority representations about planning permission appeal decisions

Following on the 1 April 2004 publication of the Scottish Executive's consultation paper *Rights of Appeal in Planning* (about third-party rights of appeal) some planning authorities made representations regarding their preference for planning appeal decisions to be taken locally by democratically elected local councillors as opposed to those decisions being taken exclusively, or almost exclusively, by the reporters on behalf of the Scottish Ministers.

Dundee City Council, for instance, submitted a petition, dated 30 April 2004, to the Scottish Parliament (reference PE740). The petition called upon the Scottish Parliament to amend the 1997 Act 'to the effect of giving the democratically elected planning authorities the final say on the planning merits of all applications [for planning permission] competently before them for determination with the current appeal provisions which pertain to [the Scottish Ministers'] reporters' decisions applying to appeals against the decisions of planning authorities'. The petition cited the August 2002 decision by one of the Scottish Ministers' reporters to allow an appeal and grant an application for planning permission for a

---

34 At para 10.55.

change of use from shop to indoor amusement centre at 60–62 Nethergate, Dundee.[35]

Dundee City Council considered that the arrangements then in place for planning permission appeals did not reflect or respect the status of planning authority decisions. It was concerned that a Scottish Ministers' reporter

- can determine the appeal as if the application for planning permission was made to the reporter in the first instance;
- was not constrained in any way from interfering with the decision locally made by the elected planning authority; and
- can change that decision where a different planning judgment is made from that made by the elected planning authority.

In contrast, any planning authority challenge to the decision of a reporter appointed by the Scottish Ministers had to be based on a point of law. It could not be based on planning merits.

Dundee City Council considered that this effectively gave an unelected civil servant the 'last bite of the cherry' in an application for planning permission and that this could not be considered to be legitimate as it amounted to a clear case of 'democratic deficit' in the planning system operating in Scotland.

Dundee City Council's suggestion, including the grounds for it, was similar to the suggestion rejected in 1988 by the Committee of the JUSTICE-All Souls Review of Administrative Law in the United Kingdom (see above).

Some might consider that Dundee City Council's analysis was flawed. First, in both national park authorities (Cairngorms National Park Authority and Loch Lomond and The Trossachs National Park Authority) those bodies taking planning application decisions could comprise not only elected members but also members appointed by the Scottish Ministers. Second, at the time Dundee City Council's petition was considered, planning appeal decisions were taken by either the Scottish Ministers, or by one of their reporters on behalf of the Scottish Ministers. The Scottish

---

35 DPEA reference PPA-180-90, Dundee City Council application reference 02/00011/COU.

Ministers, like local authority councillors, are elected and are democratically accountable.

However, Dundee City Council's representations put in focus
the principle of democratic accountability and whether the Scottish
Parliament should reaffirm the Scottish Ministers (and their officials) being empowered to decide planning permission appeals or
whether such appeals should be determined by planning authorities. As shall be seen, Dundee City Council's representations were
successful in part in that the outcome was not the wholesale transfer
of planning permission powers to planning authorities but a partial
transfer of power to committees of planning authorities, known
as 'local review bodies', to determine challenges to many 'local
development' planning application decisions.

2005 White Paper: schemes of delegation and local review bodies

The 2005 White Paper signalled the aim of extending the powers
of planning authority officers to determine 'local development'
applications. It said that a key benefit of introducing decision-
taking by local review bodies would be that the vast majority of all
appeals would henceforth be decided quickly and decided locally,
recognising that local authorities are best placed to take decisions
on local matters.

The 2005 White Paper included the proposals that:

- planning authorities be required to put in place new delegation schemes that allow planning authority officers to determine a wider range of planning applications for 'local
  developments' with a full range of decisions (including refusal
  of the application) to facilitate taking decisions quickly on
  planning applications for 'local developments';
- a committee of the planning authority would determine such
  applications falling outwith the delegated powers of planning
  officers;
- applicants for 'local developments' have the right to appeal to
  a local review body against decisions taken by planning authority officers (rather than an appeal to the Scottish Ministers);
- the local review body be made up of locally elected
  members;

- the applicant submit grounds of appeal, which would be supplied to the local review body accompanied by the case file including a copy of the planning authority officer's decision;
- only in exceptional circumstances, such as a change in national or development plan policy, will consideration extend beyond the matters contained in the planning application and related representations as considered by the planning authority officer;
- the local review body would carry out an 'independent review' of the planning authority officer's decision, 'rather than considering the proposal afresh'; and
- any challenge to the local review body's decision would be by way of a statutory appeal or judicial review.

The Scottish Executive considered that these measures, taken together, would result in a significant improvement to the planning process at the local level and a key benefit would be that the vast majority of all planning permission appeals would be decided quickly and decided locally, recognising that local authorities are best placed to take decisions on local matters.

Others might have considered that the proposed centralisation of determining the content of development plans was to be balanced by proposals to bolster local decision-making power to include determining applications for planning permission – for instance for proposed developments of up to 299 dwellings.

The analysis of responses to the 2005 White Paper recorded substantial levels of support for the proposal of a statutory scheme of delegation to officers to enable them to deal with a wider range of non-controversial planning applications. However, the analysis of responses also recorded that there were some concerns from the voluntary and community sectors that officers were less likely than members to take community views into account, and that the process was open to abuse by developers.

The responses to the 2005 White Paper proposals regarding the proposed local planning review expressed a number of points including:

- the planning authority being perceived as judge and jury – this consideration was at the heart of the government's proposals to move away from local planning authority (to central government) decision-taking in development planning and yet government was inconsistently proposing to move (away from central government) to local planning authority decision-taking in development management;

- that there would be a diminution in the quality of the development management planning system in Scotland by having decision-taking taken away from professional reporters and given to planning authority members (overwhelmingly lay people in development management) who would be subject to local pressure;
- planning authority members considering reviews would be too open to inevitable parochial pressures;
- the failure to recognise that local authorities were no longer local in size and that decisions would not be taken locally by those locally accountable (so, for instance, a decision about a proposed development in North Queensferry being taken in Glenrothes by councillors representing wards in Kirkcaldy, Cupar or elsewhere in north-east Fife would not be one taken locally by those best placed to take decisions on local matters); and
- the repeal of local authority housing benefit review bodies which considered appeals against adverse decisions taken by local authority housing officers, suggested that the 2005 White Paper proposals were not well founded.

The analysis of responses regarding proposals for local planning reviews in Scotland included statements such as:

- Of all the proposals in the 2005 White Paper package, the 'local development' category attracted the highest proportion of reservations with almost half of respondents expressing concerns. These concerns centred on the independence and competence of the proposed local member review bodies. Various alternative suggestions were made and respondents suggested there was a need for training and development in planning matters and appeal procedures for members with no expertise in that area. There were views expressed that it was likely there would be a substantial increase in member and officer workloads, and clarification sought of what was intended to be available to applicants, in terms of further appeal rights.

- Many observations queried how the local member review bodies were to be constituted and expressed serious reservations about a panel composed entirely of local members, given their likely previous involvement in planning policy and decisions. It was felt that this would make the allegation of bias, with the authority being judge and jury in its own cause, difficult to resist and would undermine public confidence in the system. Several commentators felt that the arrangement may not be compliant with Article 6 of the European Convention on Human Rights (right to a fair trial).

- There were queries regarding the availability of planning advice (with some specific concerns about architectural and ecological matters) to the local member review bodies, since officers involved in the appealed decision would, presumably, be disbarred. Some considered that, in that context, there would be a greater need for planning consultants, others that local authority lawyers could do much of the work. There was a strand of opinion which felt that the distinction between reviewing the decision and considering the proposal afresh may be difficult to maintain in practice.

- There was no consensus among respondents as to whether the proposed arrangements would speed up or slow down the process. Some respondents thought applicants might prefer the local review body route and try and trigger appeals which would lengthen the process, others believed it would merely shift delays from (the Scottish Ministers acting through) the Scottish Executive Inquiry Reporters Unit (now the DPEA) to the local authorities, who were already 'overburdened and understaffed'. The alternative view was that for the vast majority of straightforward applications local member review bodies would provide a quicker and less problematical route to a decision.

Planning etc (Scotland) Bill

The Policy Memorandum for the Bill stated, at paragraphs 146–148, that:

- the policy aim is to ensure that wide-ranging schemes of delegation are put in place, allowing officers to approve and refuse 'local development' planning applications;
- the introduction of schemes of delegation will provide a clear, accelerated process at the local level for many small-scale developments that are not controversial and are in accordance with the development plan; and
- decisions that have been taken by delegated officials will be subject to review by the planning authority – the form and procedure for such reviews will be set out in regulations.

The Financial Memorandum for the Bill indicates, at paragraphs 230, 231, 232 and 255, that:

- as many as 30 per cent of all appeals currently handled by the Scottish Ministers being determined locally by planning authorities through their local review bodies;
- the proposals to expand the scope of permitted development rights will exempt a number of minor developments (estimated to be as many as 20 per cent of the current number of applications) from the need for planning permission, with a consequent effect on the number of reviews;
- an estimated total reduction of around 60 per cent in the number of appeals being handled by the Scottish Ministers; and
- the time and cost impact of instigating, resourcing and interfacing with a local review body is likely to be roughly analogous to those of the existing planning committees.

Scottish Parliament's consideration of schemes of delegation and local planning reviews

The 10 May 2006 report of the Scottish Parliament's Communities Committee recorded that the committee:

- was of the view that a statutory provision for formal schemes of delegation to be put in place in all planning authorities will be effective in helping planning authorities manage an ever-increasing number of applications for planning permission; and

- recognised the concerns put forward by a number of bodies (including the Law Society of Scotland and the Faculty of Advocates) that a review being carried out by the same statutory body that took the initial 'local development' planning application decision may not comply with the requirements of Article 6 of the European Convention on Human Rights and called upon the Scottish Executive to note these concerns and to make every effort to ensure that the local review process is seen to be as open, transparent and robust as possible.

Principles of democratic accountability and the rule of law

The proposals to establish local review bodies can be considered in terms of the principles of democracy and the rule of law. For instance, what is the appropriate forum for the determination of the planning merits of 'local development' planning applications – the Scottish Ministers or planning authorities? Do the provisions for local review body decision-making accord with the law?

It was said by Lord Hoffmann in the House of Lords' judgment in *R v Secretary of State for the Environment, ex parte Holding and Barnes, Alconbury Developments Ltd and Legal and General Assurance Society Ltd* that:

'In a democratic country, decisions as to what the general interest requires are made by democratically elected bodies or persons accountable to them. Sometimes the subject-matter is such that Parliament can itself lay down general rules for enforcement by the courts. Taxation is a good example; Parliament decides on grounds of general interest what taxation is required and the rules according to which it should be levied. The application of those rules, to determine the liability of a particular person, is then a matter for independent and impartial tribunals such as the General or Special Commissioners or the courts. On the other hand, sometimes one cannot formulate general rules and the question of what the general interest requires has to be determined on a case by case basis. Town and country planning or road construction, in which every decision is in some respects different, are archetypal examples. In such cases Parliament may delegate the decision-making power to local democratically elected bodies or to ministers of the Crown responsible to Parliament. In that way the democratic principle is preserved.

'There is however another relevant principle which must exist in a democratic society. That is the rule of law. When ministers or officials make decisions affecting the rights of individuals, they must do so in accordance with the law. The legality of what they do must be subject to review by independent and impartial tribunals. This is reflected in the requirement in article 1 of Protocol 1 [of the European Convention on Human Rights] that a taking of property must be "subject to the conditions provided for by law". The principles of judicial review give effect to the rule of law. They ensure that administrative decisions will be taken rationally, in accordance with a fair procedure and within the powers conferred by Parliament.'[36]

The 2004 petition by Dundee City Council to the Scottish Parliament put in focus the principle of democratic accountability – the choice being whether that principle was to be observed by retaining planning permission appeals to the Scottish Ministers or by transferring the responsibility to planning authorities. Others questioned whether the proposals for local review bodies accorded with the law.

European Convention on Human Rights

The European Convention for the Protection of Human Rights and Fundamental Freedoms (sometimes referred to as the European Convention on Human Rights ('the ECHR')), Article 6 (right to a fair trial) provides procedural guarantees. ECHR Article 6(1) includes the provision that:

---

36 [2001] UKHL 23 at paras 69 and 73.

'In the determination of his civil rights and obligations . . ., everyone is entitled to a fair and public hearing within a reasonable time
by an independent and impartial tribunal established by law.'

Determination of civil rights

The right to property is a 'civil' right within the meaning of
ECHR Article 6(1). The determination of an application for planning permission is directly concerned with the way in which a
person is entitled to use land. Deciding an application for planning
permission is relevant to a person's property rights, involves the
determination of a person's civil rights and engages the rights conferred by ECHR Article 6(1).[37]

ECHR Article 6(1) guaranteed rights

ECHR Article 6(1) guarantees certain rights. Those rights can be
summarised as including the right of effective access to the courts;
the right to a fair hearing; the right to a public hearing;[38] the right
to a reasoned decision; the right to a hearing within a reasonable
period of time[39] and the right to a hearing before an independent
and impartial tribunal established by law.[40]

ECHR Article 6(1) and administrative decisions

In some instances of administrative decision-taking the European
Court has held that compliance with ECHR Article 6(1) requires a
jurisdiction to examine all questions of fact and law relevant to the
dispute either when the initial decision is taken or on appeal.

For instance *Tsfayo v United Kingdom* involved a dispute about
housing benefits where the decision-making body was a housing

---

37 See, eg, *R v Secretary of State for the Environment, ex parte Holding and Barnes,
    Alconbury Developments Ltd and General Assurance Society Ltd* [2001] UKHL
    23.
38 See Chapter 4, after the subheading 'Review procedure' regarding waiver
    of this right.
39 See, eg, *Lafarge Redland Aggregates Ltd v Scottish Ministers* 2000 SLT 1361.
40 An 'independent' tribunal is a tribunal 'which is independent of the
    executive and also of the parties'.

benefit review body ('HBRB') comprising members of the local authority which would be required to pay any housing benefit awarded.[41] The European Court of Human Rights referred to the HBRB 'deciding a simple question of fact'. It said that no special expertise was required for the decision and that the factual findings in this case could not be said to be merely incidental to the reaching of broader judgments of policy or expediency which it was for the democratically accountable authority to take. Further, it noted that the HBRB was directly connected to one of the parties to the dispute and the procedural safeguards were not adequate to overcome this fundamental lack of impartiality.

Decision-making by the HBRB did not sufficiently comply with ECHR Article 6(1) and an application for judicial review to the High Court (which had power to intervene where for instance there was no evidence to support the HBRB's factual findings, or that its findings were plainly untenable, or where the HBRB had misunderstood or been ignorant of an established and relevant fact) did not provide 'sufficiency of review' to remedy the lack of independence and impartiality at first instance.

In cases where the administrative decision involves what has been described as 'the classic exercise of administrative discretion' – that is where the relevant decision requires professional or specialist knowledge or experience and the exercise of administrative discretion pursuant to wider policy aims – such as cases relating to compulsory purchase, the requirement for a decision-making body with jurisdiction on all questions of fact and law relevant to the dispute before it does not apply. In such cases the court's restricted jurisdiction on questions of fact in a judicial review of the legality of the decision is sufficient to comply with ECHR Article 6(1).

However, judicial review of the legality of the decision will only be sufficient in such cases of the 'classic exercise of administrative discretion' if the decision on the merits which is being challenged in the courts was taken by an administrative body that follows a quasi-judicial procedure that sufficiently complies with ECHR

41 [2007] ECHR 656.

Article 6(1).[42] Therefore the manner in which the decision was arrived at is crucial.

It is the safeguards provided by the administrative decision-making process together with jurisdiction on questions of law and limited jurisdiction on questions of fact of the judicial body determining a person's civil rights and obligations which, taken together, provide a sufficiency of review that is compliant with ECHR Article 6(1).

The relevant law was described succinctly by Baroness Hale of Richmond in *R (Wright and Others) v Secretary of State for Health* as follows:

'It is a well-known principle that decisions which determine civil rights and obligations may be made by the administrative authorities, provided that there is then access to an independent and impartial tribunal which exercises "full jurisdiction": *Bryan v United Kingdom* (1995) 21 EHRR 342. . . . What amounts to "full jurisdiction" varies according to the nature of the decision being made. It does not always require access to a court or tribunal even for the determination of disputed issues of fact. Much depends upon the subject-matter of the decision and the quality of the initial decision-making process. If there is a "classic exercise of administrative discretion", even though determinative of civil rights and obligations, and there are a number of safeguards to ensure that the procedure is in fact both fair and impartial, then judicial review may be adequate to supply the necessary access to a court, even if there is no jurisdiction to examine the factual merits of the case. The planning system is a classic example (*Alconbury*); so too, it has been held, is the allocation of "suitable" housing to the homeless (*Runa Begum*); but allowing councillors to decide whether there was a good excuse for a late claim to housing benefit was not (*Tsfayo*).'[43]

---

42 See, eg, *Bryan v United Kingdom* (1995) 21 EHRR 342 followed in *R v The Secretary of State for the Environment, ex parte Holding and Barnes, Alconbury Developments Ltd and General Assurance Society Ltd* [2001] UKHL 23; *County Properties Ltd v Scottish Ministers* 2001 SLT 1125; and *Runa Begum v London Borough of Tower Hamlets* [2003] UKHL 5.

43 [2009] UKHL 3 at para 23.

Bryan v United Kingdom

In the seminal case of *Bryan v United Kingdom*[44] Mr Bryan appealed to the Secretary of State against a planning enforcement notice requiring him to demolish two buildings erected without planning permission on his land. His grounds of appeal included (a) planning permission ought to be granted for those buildings and (b) that the matters alleged in the planning enforcement notice did not constitute a breach of planning control because the buildings were permitted development in terms of the Town and Country Planning General Development Order 1988.[45] Section 174(2) of the Town and Country Planning Act 1990 empowered the inspector to consider all matters on that appeal, whether they related to facts or to law. The inspector appointed by the Secretary of State held a local public inquiry and dismissed those grounds of appeal.

Appeal to the High Court

Mr Bryan appealed against the inspector's decision under section 289 of the Town and Country Planning Act 1990. That section provides that an appeal may be made to the High Court on a point of law. It was agreed that the High Court's review could consider whether a decision or inference based on a finding of fact is perverse or irrational. The High Court could also give a remedy if the inspector's decision was such that there was no evidence to support a particular finding of fact; or the decision was made by reference to irrelevant factors or without regard to relevant factors or without proper regard to relevant factors; or the decision was made for an improper purpose, in a procedurally unfair manner or in a manner which breached any governing legislation.

The High Court did not have jurisdiction to examine all questions of fact. It had no power to receive further evidence on primary facts.

Mr Bryan's challenge to the inspector's reasoning about whether planning permission ought to be granted 'concerned questions

---

44 (1995) 21 EHRR 342.
45 SI 1988/1813.

which indeed call for respect on the "grounds of expediency" as
they involved the application of the panoply of policy matters such
as development plans, and the facts that the property was situated
in a green belt and in a Conservation Area.' The permitted development rights challenge 'raised matters of a more factual nature in
that they would have gone directly to questions of whether Mr
Bryan had erected a building which fell within the General Development Order, and so had the benefit of deemed planning permission.' Mr Bryan did not maintain the permitted development
rights challenge in his appeal in the High Court. His appeal was
dismissed by the High Court in March 1991 and leave to appeal
was refused in June 1991.

ECHR complaint

In October 1991 Mr Bryan complained to the European Commission of Human Rights. His complaints included that the review
undertaken by the High Court of the inspector's decision was not
of sufficient scope to comply with ECHR Article 6(1).

Determination of a 'civil right'

There was no dispute that the enforcement notice appeal proceedings involved a determination of Mr Bryan's 'civil rights'. The
right of property is clearly a 'civil' right within the meaning of
ECHR Article 6. The enforcement notice issued by the local
authority and the subsequent enforcement proceedings were
directly concerned with the way in which Mr Bryan was entitled
to use his land. Therefore the proceedings in the *Bryan* case determined a 'civil right'.

Fair hearing

The European Court of Human Rights held that the proceedings
before the inspector ensured Mr Bryan a fair hearing for the
purposes of ECHR Article 6(1).

   The court referred to the uncontested safeguards attending the
procedure before the inspector; the quasi-judicial character of the
decision-making process; the duty incumbent on any of the Secre-

tary of State's inspectors to exercise independent judgment; the requirement that inspectors must not be subject to any improper influence; the stated mission of the Planning Inspectorate to uphold the principles of openness, fairness and impartiality. Further, the court noted that any shortcomings in relation to these safeguards could have been subject to a review by the High Court.

Independent and impartial tribunal

An issue that had to be considered was whether the inspector constituted an 'independent and impartial tribunal established by law'.

The court held that the function of the inspector was to determine matters within his competence on the basis of rules of law, following proceedings conducted in a prescribed manner. He therefore came within the concept of 'tribunal' in the substantive sense of the expression used in ECHR Article 6(1). Further the tribunal was one 'established by law' – namely the Town and Country Planning Act 1990.

In order to establish whether a body can be considered to be 'independent' regard must be had to matters such as the manner of appointment of its members and to its term of office, to the guarantees against outside public pressures and to the question whether the body presents an appearance of independence.

Although the inspector was required to decide Mr Bryan's planning enforcement appeal in a quasi-judicial, independent and impartial, as well as fair, manner, the Secretary of State could at any time issue a direction to revoke the power of the inspector to decide an appeal. In the context of planning appeals the very existence of this power available to the Executive, whose own policies may be in issue, was enough to deprive the inspector of the requisite appearance of independence, notwithstanding the limited exercise of the power by the Secretary of State in practice and irrespective of whether its exercise was or could have been in issue in Mr Bryan's case. For this reason alone, the review by an inspector did not of itself satisfy the ECHR Article 6(1) requirements, despite the existence of various safeguards customarily associated with an 'independent and impartial' tribunal.

Review by the High Court and ECHR Article 6(1) compliance

The planning appeal proceedings before the inspector did not comply with ECHR Article 6(1) because of the inspector's lack of independence. Therefore the issue in Mr Bryan's case was whether the review by the High Court was sufficient to remedy the lack of independence at the first instance.

An appeal to the High Court was only on points of law. The review by the High Court was not capable of embracing all aspects of the inspector's decision about the planning enforcement notice. In particular there was no rehearing of the grounds of appeal submitted to the inspector; the High Court could not substitute its own decision on the merits for that of the inspector and its jurisdiction over facts was limited.

However, apart from the classic grounds of unlawfulness under English law (going to such issues as fairness, procedural impropriety, independence and impartiality), the inspector's decision could have been quashed by the High Court if it had been made by reference to irrelevant factors or without regard to relevant factors, or if the evidence relied upon by the inspector was not capable of supporting a finding of fact, or if the decision was based on an inference from facts which was perverse or irrational, in the sense that no inspector properly directing himself would have drawn such an inference.

In assessing the sufficiency of the review available to an applicant on appeal to the High Court it was also necessary to have regard to such matters as the subject matter of the decision appealed against, the manner in which that decision was arrived at, and the context of the dispute, including the desired and actual grounds of appeal. The European Court of Human Rights drew attention to the 'uncontested safeguards attending the procedure before the inspector: the quasi-judicial character of the decision-making process; the duty incumbent on each inspector to exercise independent judgment; the requirement that inspectors must not be subject to any improper influence; the stated mission of the Inspectorate to uphold the principles of openness, fairness and impartiality.' Any alleged shortcomings in relation to procedural and other safeguards could be the subject of review by the High Court.

The European Court of Human Rights noted that in Mr Bryan's case there was no dispute as to primary facts. Nor was any challenge made at the hearing in the High Court to the factual inferences drawn by the inspector, following Mr Bryan abandoning his objection to the inspector's reasoning about whether the two buildings were permitted development in terms of the Town and Country Planning General Development Order 1988. The High Court had jurisdiction to entertain the remaining ground of Mr Bryan's appeal and the submissions on his behalf were dealt with point by point. These submissions went essentially to questions of policy matters and the fact that Mr Bryan's property was situated in the green belt and a Conservation Area.

Further, and importantly, the European Court of Human Rights stated that, if Mr Bryan had wanted to question the inspector's findings of fact, there would still have been no breach of ECHR Article 6(1). Although the High Court could not have substituted its own findings of fact for those of the inspector, it had the power to satisfy itself that the inspector's findings of fact or the inferences based on them were neither perverse nor irrational. The court noted that such an approach by an appeal tribunal on questions of fact can reasonably be expected in specialised areas of law (such as town and country planning), particularly where the facts have been established in the course of a quasi-judicial procedure governed by many of the safeguards required by ECHR Article 6(1). The court noted that:

- this approach was frequently a feature in the systems of judicial control of administrative decisions found throughout the Council of Europe Member States; and
- in this instance, the subject matter of the inspector's contested decision was a typical example of the exercise of discretionary judgment in the regulation of citizens' conduct in the sphere of town and country planning.

The scope of review of the High Court complied with ECHR Article 6(1). Accordingly the remedies available to Mr Bryan in relation to his complaints satisfied the requirements of ECHR Article 6(1).

Importance of the Bryan decision

It follows from the *Bryan* decision that, in cases of 'the classic exercise of administrative discretion' where the administrative body is not an 'independent and impartial tribunal' and where the decision of the administrative body does not involve a quasi-judicial procedure that sufficiently complies with ECHR Article 6(1), then what ECHR Article 6(1) requires is an appeal for a final decision on the merits of a person's civil rights and obligations before an 'independent and impartial tribunal', if and to the extent that it is such an appeal that the applicant wishes to make.

In cases of 'the classic exercise of administrative discretion' judicial review of the legality of the administrative decision will only be sufficient where the initial decision on the merits involves a quasi-judicial procedure that sufficiently complies with ECHR Article 6(1). The manner in which the decision was arrived at is important. For instance, in the *Alconbury* decision it is clear, in relation to findings in fact and the inferences from fact, that the relevant safeguards (including those provided by the public inquiries and related post-inquiry procedures) were essential to the acceptance of a limited review of fact by the courts. Therefore the availability of judicial review at the end of a decision-making process does not of itself guarantee that the process is ECHR Article 6(1) compliant.

Scrutiny of provisions about local review bodies

The December 2005 Policy Memorandum for the Planning etc (Scotland) Bill:

- noted that an applicant for planning permission has a right of appeal either to a planning authority (through its local review body) or to the Scottish Ministers and that the Bill removed an applicant's current right to a hearing and limited the introduction of new matters; and
- stated 'there will remain a right of legal challenge to the Court of Session, and in our view this ensures that the [proposed appeals regime is] compliant with [ECHR] Article 6.'[46]

---

46 At para 249.

Concerns were reiterated about the proposals for local review bodies and ECHR Article 6(1) compliance in meetings of the Scottish Parliament's Communities Committee in 2006 to consider the Bill. The Scottish Executive, echoing the Bill's Policy Memorandum, stated 'the protection of having an appeal to the court on a point of law makes the system ECHR compliant on an holistic view.'[47] It was recognised that any proper assessment could only be made once further details, which were to be provided in subsidiary legislation, were available.[48]

In February 2008 a public consultation *Modernising Planning Appeals* was carried out on draft regulations including those for 'local development' schemes of delegation and 'local development' reviews.[49] The analysis of consultation responses was published in December 2008.[50] The key themes from the responses were about independence and impartiality; consistency of approach and transparency and fairness. Some amendments were made to the draft regulations following upon that consultation.

In that consultation concerns were reiterated about whether the proposals for local review bodies were ECHR Article 6(1) compliant and, in turn, lawful.

The Executive Note published along with the Town and Country Planning (Schemes of Delegation and Local Review Procedure) (Scotland) Regulations 2008[51] ('the 2008 Regulations') recorded that in consultation a range of stakeholders (including the Law Society, the Faculty of Advocates and the Administrative Justice and Tribunals Council Scottish Committee) raised concerns about the principle of local review bodies and the potential for them not to work effectively. Some of these concerns related to the

---

47 Lynda Towers, Office of the Solicitor to the Scottish Executive, Communities Committee, Official Report, 8 February 2006, column 3027.

48 John Watchman, Planning Sub-Committee of the Law Society of Scotland, Communities Committee, 1 February 2006, column 2957–8.

49 www.gov.scot/Publications/2008/02/13104117/0

50 www.gov.scot/Publications/2008/12/02095250/0 and www.gov.scot/Publications/2008/12/02095331/0

51 SSI 2008/433.

extent to which a local review will provide a fair or independent hearing, whether it will demonstrate impartiality or provide a process that the general public will have confidence in. That note recorded:

> 'Scottish Government remains of the view that the local review is part of a process that complies with the European Convention on Human Rights.'[52]

It is somewhat surprising therefore that when the 2008 Regulations were being scrutinised in January 2009 by the Subordinate Legislation Committee of the Scottish Parliament that relevant questions about ECHR Article 6(1) compliance were not raised.

This can be contrasted with the approach adopted at the same time by the Subordinate Legislation Committee of the Scottish Parliament in considering the Town and Country Planning (Appeals) (Scotland) Regulations 2008.[53] The committee asked a question about ECHR Article 6(1) compliance and apparently accepted the Scottish Government's response that as regards the details of secondary legislation for appeals to the Scottish Ministers:

> 'It is recognised in the case law that the Scottish Ministers, or indeed a person appointed by them to consider the case, do not constitute the independent tribunal within the meaning of article 6(1) of the ECHR. It is the access to the Court of Session under sections 237 to 239 which supplies the necessary entitlement to a fair and public hearing by an independent and impartial tribunal. The changes made by the Regulations or indeed the 2006 Act do not alter the right to a hearing in the Court of Session nor do they alter the scope of the Court of Session's jurisdiction.'

That response apparently fails to acknowledge that, absent 'an independent tribunal', a quasi-judicial process that sufficiently complies with ECHR Article 6(1) may be required in the initial decision-making process and it fails to recognise the importance of the manner in which the decision will be taken including any attendant safeguards about findings of fact or the evaluation of

---

52 www.legislation.gov.uk/ssi/2008/433/pdfs/ssien_20080433_en.pdf
53 SSI 2008/434.

facts. The availability of judicial review at the end of a decision-making process does not of itself guarantee that the process is ECHR Article 6(1) compliant.

Further, the view of the Scottish Executive, and subsequently the Scottish Government, apparently fails to recognise the particular context for the court decisions in the *Bryan* and *Alconbury* cases. These were concerned directly with issues which affect only a small number of cases: a decision to be taken by the Secretary of State following receipt of an inspector's report informed by matters being considered through a public inquiry process.

Moreover, in addition to there being a public inquiry before an inspector:

- either the facts found by the inspector must be accepted by the Secretary of State or, if the Secretary of State differed from the inspector on any matter of fact and was for that reason disposed to disagree with the inspector's recommendation, the Secretary of State was prohibited from coming to a decision at variance with the inspector's recommendation without affording parties an opportunity to make representations about the Secretary of State's reasons for the disagreement; and
- the decision would subsequently be taken by the Secretary of State.

Importantly, the courts considered that in deciding the questions of primary fact or fact and degree and drawing conclusions and inferences from those facts, an inspector (as an expert tribunal acting in a quasi-judicial manner) was sufficiently independent to make it unnecessary for the courts to have a broad jurisdiction to review decisions on questions of fact.

Provisions about schemes of delegation and local planning reviews

The relevant legislation about schemes of delegation and local review bodies was first included in sections 43A and 43B of the 1997 Act and the 2008 Regulations. Scottish Government guidance was first set out in its Circular 7/2009: *Schemes of Delegation and Local Reviews.*[54]

As noted below, following a public consultation on miscellaneous amendments to the planning system launched in March 2012,[55] and consideration of the analysis of the consultation responses,[56] that legislation was amended in 2013. Current guidance is set out in Scottish Government Circular 5/2013: *Schemes of Delegation and Local Reviews.*[57] Further 'best practice' guidance has been issued by the Local Review Body Forum.[58]

From 6 April 2009, the provisions in the 2008 Regulations about 'local development' schemes of delegation came into force. These regulations prohibited the delegation of 'local development' planning applications that are made by the planning authority or a member of that authority or where the authority has a financial or ownership interest in the application land. The Scottish Government described the prohibition as a 'safeguard' and presumably it was also included to engender public trust in the planning system. However, that prohibition was removed by the Town and Country Planning (Schemes of Delegation and Local Review Procedure) (Scotland) Regulations 2013 ('the 2013 Regulations').[59]

Therefore planning authorities are now empowered, but are not required, to delegate decisions about 'local development' planning applications made by the planning authority or a member of that authority or where the authority has a financial or ownership interest in the application land.

Since 3 August 2009, where an applicant requires it of a relevant planning authority in Scotland (the 33 planning authorities are the

---

54 www.gov.scot/Publications/2009/07/07115301/0
55 www.gov.scot/Publications/2012/03/5577/downloads
56 www.gov.scot/Publications/2012/09/9618/downloads and www.gov.scot/Publications/2012/08/1764/downloads
57 www.gov.scot/Publications/2013/12/8902
58 www.gov.scot/Topics/Built-Environment/planning/aboutappeals
59 SSI 2013/157.

32 councils[60] and the Loch Lomond and The Trossachs National Park Authority[61]) the relevant planning authority is empowered (through a committee comprising at least three members known as the 'local review body') to conduct a review of:

- decisions taken by one of their officers appointed by virtue of a scheme of delegation made under section 43A(1) of the 1997 Act to refuse or to grant subject to conditions an application for planning permission for a development within the hierarchy of developments category of 'local development' or for consent, agreement or approval required by a condition imposed on such a grant of planning permission; or
- an appointed officer's failure to issue a decision on such a 'local development' application within the prescribed period (normally two months or, from 2 February 2013 such extended period as agreed in writing between the applicant and the appointed officer) which failure is deemed to be a decision to refuse the application;

and to uphold, reverse or vary the decision reviewed.

Section 43A(17) of the 1997 Act provides that where a requirement for a review is made by virtue of section 43A(8)(c) of the 1997 Act and the planning authority has not considered the review within such period as prescribed, the planning authority is deemed to have decided to refuse the application and the applicant can make an appeal to the Scottish Ministers.

Two amendments have been made to the relevant legislation, namely:

- From 2 February 2013 the Public Services Reform (Planning) (Local Review Procedure) (Scotland) Order 2013 (SSI 2013/

---

60 Local Government etc (Scotland) Act 1994, s 2.

61 National Parks (Scotland) Act 2000, s 10; Loch Lomond and The Trossachs National Park Designation, Transitional and Consequential Provisions (Scotland) Order 2002 (SSI 2002/201) and Loch Lomond and The Trossachs National Park Designation, Transitional and Consequential Provisions (Scotland) Order 2002 Modification Order 2010 (SSI 2010/ 347).

24) amended section 43A(8)(c) of the 1997 Act to enable the applicant and the appointed officer to agree in writing to extend the prescribed period (if the proposed application requires an environmental impact assessment the period is four months – otherwise the period is two months after the validation date) which means that such an extension, in effect, allows the planning authority more time to take a decision at first instance while preserving the three-month period for requiring a review on the grounds of non-determination.

- From 30 June 2013 the 2013 Regulations amended the provisions of the 1997 Act giving an applicant the right to appeal to Scottish Ministers in circumstances where a local review body does not determine a review and the case is automatically deemed to be refused. The 2013 Regulations extended the 'non-determination' or 'deemed refusal' period of two months set out in the 2008 Regulations to three months which, in effect, extends the period of time in which a local review body could determine a review and, failing such a determination, the applicant could appeal to the Scottish Ministers.

Circular 5/2013: *Schemes of Delegation and Local Reviews* provides a narrative about the current law and highlights the changes to the original legislation. However, it is noteworthy that there is an absence of any meaningful guidance about the operation of local review bodies in practice.

The Local Review Body Forum's best practice guidance provides more detailed information relevant to local planning reviews in Scotland. Further, the DPEA has also issued guidance to its reporters (for instance *Reporter Guidance Note 16: New matters and the submission of documents, material or evidence*) which may be useful for those involved with local planning reviews in Scotland.[62]

---

62 www.gov.scot/Topics/Built-Environment/planning/Appeals/howwework/
   guidanceforreporters

Reactions to the introduction of planning authority reviews

What reactions have there been to the introduction of planning authority reviews of 'local development' planning application decisions delegated to planning officers for determination?

Planning authority reviews elsewhere in the United Kingdom

In November 2007 a bill was introduced into the Westminster Parliament with proposed reforms for the planning regime south of the border.[63] That bill was the basis for what ultimately became the Planning Act 2008. Part 9 of the Planning Bill included requirements for local planning authorities to make arrangements for certain planning applications to be determined by officers, with a right of review by members of local planning authorities rather than a right of appeal to the Secretary of State. However, following strong opposition, in particular a campaign by the Royal Town Planning Institute, those provisions were abandoned.

Neither the 2013 Northern Ireland Assembly Planning Bill nor the 2014 Welsh Government Planning (Wales) Bill include provisions about planning applications being determined by officers with a right to apply for a review by members of local planning authorities.

Audit Scotland

In September 2011 Audit Scotland stated that local review bodies were 'largely untested'.

Administrative Justice and Tribunals Council ('the AJTC')

In February 2012 the Scottish Committee of the Administrative Justice and Tribunals Council ('SCAJTC') published its review of the operation of local review bodies in *Modernising Planning – Local*

---

63 www.publications.parliament.uk/pa/cm200708/cmbills/011/2008011.pdf

Review Bodies.[64] That paper cited an article 'Planning reforms in Scotland',[65] in which Professor Mark Poustie indicated that Lord Hoffmann in *Runa Begum* doubted whether the procedural safeguard element is so important (in the 'normal case' of an administrative decision 'fairness and rationality should be enough') and indicated that the key issue may simply be the availability of a judicial review-type procedure at the end of the process. Professor Poustie noted that this approach has not been confirmed by the European Court of Human Rights. He then stated as regards the system of local planning reviews in Scotland:

> '[What] is more problematic is the overt lack of independence. Thus, although the [local review] body will consist of elected members who have not been involved in the earlier decision, nevertheless those elected members are part of the same body. This raises rather different questions than would be the case if the "appeal" were simply an internal administrative review to a senior officer as may be found, for example, in homelessness legislation [which was the legislation considered in *Runa Begum*]. There may also be difficulties in preserving impartiality simply because it will be difficult to ensure that members have no knowledge of the appeal or limited contact with the officer. This does not seem to provide anywhere near the same level of safeguards as were identified as being important in *Bryan*. It may well be that these potential problems simply cannot be cured by a judicial review-type procedure.'[66]

The SCAJTC paper also made reference to the response by the Faculty of Advocates to the 2005 White Paper which highlighted that the reason the challenges in both the *Bryan v UK* and *Alconbury* cases failed was because of the quasi-judicial nature of the public inquiry process. The Faculty of Advocates emphasised the importance of the fact that evidence is led and cross-examined and findings of fact are made, and considered that:

> 'Should less robust methods be put in place, particularly when

---

64 ajtc.justice.gov.uk/docs/Modernising_Planning_2_-_LRB_Working_Paper.pdf

65 [2007] JPL 489.

66 [2007] JPL 489 at 510.

there are disputes of fact or inferences from facts, then either the scope of judicial review would have to widen or else the risk is increased that the system is not [ECHR] Article 6 compliant.'

SCAJTC noted and articulated its concerns about inconsistencies in the interpretation of relevant legislation and guidance in each of the following areas:

'(1) The extent to which the function of the LRB is to determine an appeal *de novo* or a more restricted review of the appointed officer's decision.

(2) The freedom of the LRB to determine its own process on an ad-hoc case by case basis.

(3) The role of planning and legal advisors to the LRB.

(4) The approach to site visits.

(5) Schemes of delegation under [the 1997 Act] and potential conflict with a local authority's general scheme of delegation to committees [under the Local Government (Scotland) Act 1973].

(6) The introduction of new material.

(7) The delegation of decision letters and conditions to officers.

(8) The scope of what may amount to a "material consideration" justifying departure from local planning policies.'

The SCAJTC concluded:

'The principle of independence of the tribunal from the decision maker is an essential element of a fair system. Equally essential is the requirement of independent and impartial decision makers who have been properly trained. Both of these essential features of a fair tribunal are lacking in the current [local review body] system and we consider that the poor practice and flawed decision making observed in this limited scrutiny [of local review bodies] arise in consequence of these basic flaws.'

The SCAJTC set out its belief that the criticisms that it had previously made about education appeal committees, valuation appeals committees and police appeal tribunals should also be applied to the structure and operation of local planning reviews in Scotland.

In its August 2012 report *Right to Appeal*[67] the SCAJTC recommended the establishment of a national tribunal which would hear

---

67 ajtc.justice.gov.uk/docs/decisons_with_no_appeal_web_final.pdf

appeals from routine decisions by planning authorities. Local review bodies would remain in existence but there would be the possibility of an appeal from their decisions to a national, environmental tribunal. Its scope and jurisdiction would need to be defined but it would be independent of the local authority and would be a part of the Scottish Tribunals Service.

Practitioner reflections on local planning reviews

Recorded reflections of members of the Royal Incorporation of Architects in Scotland ('RIAS') about local planning review disclose, in summary, the perception of an apparent lack of fairness and transparency in local planning reviews in Scotland. The RIAS is seeking to change the local review body system.[68]

Some comments about the new development management regime

More than five years have elapsed since the new development management regime came into force. It might now be appropriate to offer some comments about that regime including local planning reviews in Scotland.

It is important to recognise that the proposed reforms envisaged not only legislative change but non-legislative changes including administrative changes. These non-legislative changes included, for instance, the use of 'processing agreements' (as a project management tool). They also included the aim of delivering 'culture change in planning' – which recognised the need to re-energise the planning profession, allied principally with elected members and senior management in local government recognising the importance of planning. Clearly the most significant success in the non-legislative changes relates to greater use of e-planning. E-planning has improved transparency in planning and access to planning materials. However e-planning is not a panacea. For instance, it has

---

68 S McIntosh, 'Practitioner reflections on local review bodies' (2014) 161 SPEL 4.

to be recognised that there are significant numbers of people within our communities who do not have access to the necessary facilities or the necessary skills to make use of e-planning. Further, sometimes there is no substitute for examining the application drawings etc because it may be extremely difficult, if not impossible, to properly do so via a computer screen.

Local review bodies and ECHR Article 6(1) compliance

At the time of writing the issue of administrative decision-taking by local review bodies and ECHR Article 6(1) compliance has not been the subject of any court decision. The statutory appeal in *Carroll v Scottish Borders Council*:

> 'made plain that the appeal was not presented as a challenge to the legislative provisions which regulate the decision-making processes of [local review bodies]. Rather, the challenge is made on grounds of failure to take into account material considerations, failure properly to interpret and apply relevant planning policies, irrationality, failure to consider proportionality, breach of natural justice and failure to give adequate reasons.'[69]

However, it seems inevitable that the issue of ECHR Article 6(1) compliance will be raised at some time in the courts. It is anticipated that the relevant provisions of the 1997 Act and the 2013 Regulations will be considered; particular attention will be paid to the manner in which local review body decisions are arrived at and the matter of safeguards in relation to findings of fact and the evaluation of facts, and an assessment will be made about whether the court's limited jurisdiction to review facts provides a 'sufficiency of review' to remedy a lack of an 'independent and impartial tribunal'.

Supervision of local review bodies

The comments noted above by SCAJTC and by RIAS members highlight the need for a formal system of supervision of local review bodies.

69 [2014] CSOH 6 at para [3].

The Scottish Government publishes details of the number of applications made to local review bodies, the average time in weeks for a decision by local review bodies and the percentage of cases where the appointed officer's decision is upheld.

Is this information considered to provide an adequate oversight of local review bodies and their decision-making?

The statistics for 2013–14 show that local review bodies across Scotland take an average of about 12 weeks to determine an application which is the subject of a notice of review. However, performance varies across the country. The average time taken by planning authorities to determine applications varies from five to 31 weeks. Authorities with a similar workload (of about 20 LRB applications in that reporting year) have average decision-making times which vary markedly – from about seven weeks (Angus Council and Moray Council) to more than 14 weeks (Dumfries and Galloway Council and East Ayrshire Council).

Improved service under the new development management regime?

What about the aim of delivering an improved, quicker and more effective planning service?

The planning landscape has changed considerably since the 2005 White Paper. For instance there has been a significant drop in the number of planning applications and a significant increase in planning application fees.

The number of planning permission applications determined annually has fallen from over 56,000 in 2004–05 (the last reporting year before the publication of the 2005 White Paper), to over 47,000 in 2008–09 (the last reporting year before the introduction of the new development management system) to about 30,000 in 2013–14 (the last reporting year). This dramatic slump in the number of applications determined can be explained in part by the change in economic conditions and, more recently, the extension of permitted development rights (which removed the need in a significant number of cases to apply for planning permission).

Planning fees have increased substantially. In 2004 the minimum planning fee was £240 and the maximum fee was £12,000; before the development management regime was reformed in 2009 the minimum fee was £290 and the maximum fee was £14,500; and from 1 November 2014 the minimum fee is £401 and the maximum fee is £20,055. Since the new development management scheme was introduced in 2009 there has been an increase in fees of over 35 per cent.

Quicker, better quality and more local planning permission decisions?

The 2005 White Paper said that the proposed planning regime reforms will improve the speed and efficiency of the process while maintaining and enhancing quality in decision-making and in the outcomes on the ground.

There has been an increase in the percentage of planning permission applications being determined by local authority officers under delegated powers. The percentage of planning applications determined under delegated powers has increased from about 84 per cent in 2004–05, to around 88 per cent in 2008–09, to about 93 per cent in 2013–14.

However, the exceptions in both the 1997 Act and the schemes of delegation for 'local development' applications determine whether an application will be decided by planning authority committee (and potentially, on appeal, by the Scottish Ministers) or the planning authority (through its local review body).

Section 43A of the 1997 Act provides that the planning authority may decide to determine a 'local development' planning application which would otherwise fall to be determined by the authority's appointed officer. Any such decision must include a statement of the reason(s) for which it has been taken and a copy of the decision must be served on the applicant.

Schemes of delegation vary across Scotland. The terms of the delegation are primarily a matter for the authorities. One common exception is where, for instance, the authority's appointed officer is minded to grant the 'local development' application but there are a specified number of objections to the proposed development or an objection by a statutory consultee. In these circumstances the application cannot properly be determined by the appointed officer and the decision on the application is potentially one that will be determined by the Scottish Ministers on appeal.

The DPEA (and its predecessor the Scottish Executive Inquiry Reporters Unit) received 894 planning permission appeals in 2004–05 and 1,049 planning permission appeals in 2008–09. Following the introduction of the new development management regime the number of planning permission appeals received in the full reporting years are 563 in 2010–11; 607 in 2011–12; 493 in 2012–13; and 427 in 2013–14. In those four full reporting years the local review bodies have received, respectively, 529, 601, 537 and 543 notices for review.

One feature that is notable is the number of planning permission appeals received by the DPEA, since the local planning review system was introduced, where it has been decided there was no jurisdiction. In the first four full reporting years there have been about 150 cases where an appeal was made and the Scottish Ministers had 'no remit'. In most, if not all, of these cases the application would have fallen within the jurisdiction of a local review body.

There are more decisions being taken by the planning authority and therefore there is greater local accountability. However, at what cost?

In general an appeal decision taken by one of the Scottish Ministers' reporters is likely to be issued earlier and at less cost than a decision taken by three members of a planning authority, with support from a planning adviser and a legal adviser, at a local review body meeting and issued at a later date (usually within 21 days of the meeting at which the decision is taken).

A better local planning service?

The reform of the planning system was supposed to deliver a better local planning service.

Despite, for instance, in 2013–14 about 93 per cent of the planning permission applications being determined by officers under delegated powers, a significantly reduced number of applications made annually (down from over 50,000 to around 30,000), and the increasing use of e-planning and project management tools such as 'processing agreements', the average times taken by planning authorities across Scotland to determine post-August 2009 planning applications are about:

- 11 weeks to determine planning applications for 'local developments';
- 15 weeks to determine 'local development' planning applications for housing developments;
- 35 weeks to determine planning applications for 'major developments'; and
- 42 weeks to determine 'major development' planning applications for housing developments.

It may not be unconnected that from 30 June 2014 section 252 of the 1997 Act has been amended (by section 55 of the Regulatory Reform (Scotland) Act 2014) to empower the Scottish Ministers to make provision for different planning application fees where the Scottish Ministers are satisfied that the functions of the planning authority are not being, or have not been, performed satisfactorily.

Chapter 2

Schemes of Delegation

Over 90 per cent of all planning permission applications are determined by officers on behalf of their planning authorities. The remaining applications are determined by members of the planning authorities either at a committee meeting of the authority, including a meeting of a local review body, or at a meeting of the authority itself. Decisions by members of a planning authority are almost always informed by a report prepared by planning authority officers about the proposed development.

Planning authorities delegate specific decision-making powers to their officers by 'schemes of delegation'. These are currently made under:

- section 56 of the Local Government (Scotland) Act 1973 ('the 1973 Act'); and
- section 43A of the 1997 Act and the Town and Country Planning (Schemes of Delegation and Local Review Procedure) (Scotland) Regulations 2013 ('the 2013 Regulations').[1]

Planning authorities are required to prepare and adopt, publish, and keep under review their schemes of delegation made under section 43A of the 1997 Act. Across Scotland there is significant variation in the provisions of 1997 Act schemes of delegation. Until recently the Scottish Government assisted the public (including applicants for planning permission and their agents) by providing a webpage with links to the relevant 1997 Act schemes of delega-

---

1 SSI 2013/157.

tion.[2] However, it is now necessary to check the relevant planning authority website for the current adopted scheme of delegation.

1973 Act discharge of functions

Section 56 of the 1973 Act provides:

'**Arrangements for discharge of functions by local authorities.**

(1) Subject to any express provision contained in this Act or any Act passed after this Act, a local authority may arrange for the discharge of any of their functions by a committee of the authority, a sub-committee, an officer of the authority or by any other local authority in Scotland.

(2) Where by virtue of this section any function of a local authority may be discharged by any committee or sub-committee of theirs, then, unless the local authority otherwise direct—

(a) a committee may arrange for the discharge of any of those functions by a sub-committee or an officer of the authority; and

(b) the sub-committee, whether assigned the discharge of functions by the authority or by a committee, may arrange for the discharge of any such functions by an officer of the authority.'

The section makes further provisions: for discharge of functions by another local authority;[3] allowing the authority itself to discharge functions even when they have been delegated;[4] for joint committees with other local authorities;[5] and other provisions, which (with one exception noted below) are not relevant here, relating to when a local authority can delegate its functions and when it cannot do so.[6]

The 1973 Act is fundamental to understanding how local authorities can operate, including when they operate as a planning

---

2 www.gov.scot/Topics/Built-Environment/planning/aboutappeals

3 Local Government (Scotland) Act 1973 ('1973 Act'), s 56(3).

4 1973 Act, s 56(4).

5 1973 Act, s 56(5).

6 1973 Act, ss 56(6), (6A), (7), (8), (9), (10), (14) and (15).

authority. Put simply, a local authority can, under the 1973 Act, carry out its functions (including taking decisions) by three main routes, namely by:

- the local authority meeting as a whole body (the 'full council');
- a local authority committee or sub-committee; or
- local authority officers being delegated to do or decide certain things on behalf of the local authority.

Of the exceptions to that rule, the only exception worth noting here is in section 56(6A) of the 1973 Act. It provides that a local authority's function of determining an application for planning permission for a development of a class mentioned in section 38A(1) of the 1997 Act shall be discharged only by the authority. This relates to those planning permission applications for 'major developments which are significantly contrary to the development plan' and 'national developments'. These applications require a pre-determination hearing.[7]

In all other respects, all planning decisions could be taken by the council meeting in full session; by a planning committee or sub-committee; or by officers appointed by the council. Each of these options has advantages and disadvantages and, in the case of most authorities, the reality is that planning decisions generally are taken in a mixture of ways.

Full council meetings, particularly in the case of the larger councils, concern themselves mainly with the major strategic decisions which councils require to take, such as the setting of the annual budget and political business to do with the operation of the council as a whole. The full council is not always the right place for the determination of applications for planning permission for proposed smaller scale developments. As noted above, section 56(6A) of the 1973 Act reserves to the full council meeting decisions on applications for planning permission for 'major developments which are significantly contrary to the development plan' and for 'national developments'. The development plan comprises in the

---

7 1997 Act, s 38A and Town and Country Planning (Development Management Procedure) (Scotland) Regulations 2013 (SSI 2013/155), reg 27.

city regions of Aberdeen, Dundee, Edinburgh and Glasgow a strategic development plan and a local development plan.[8] Elsewhere there is only a local development plan.

Most councils have a planning committee, or sub-committee, or more than one of them. Although they can be smaller in number of members and allow a degree of expertise and specialisation among the elected members, inevitably, given the requirements for reduction of agendas and papers and councillors' other commitments, they can only meet so often.

Accordingly, applications for planning permission are usually decided at committee if the scale and importance of the proposed development is considered to give rise to a need for a degree of democratic scrutiny and legitimacy. A committee or sub-committee of a local authority would not normally be considered to be an appropriate place for the day-to-day planning decisions. There has always been a view that the smallest scale planning permission applications, including the so-called householder applications, could generally be dealt with outwith a committee context unless they were especially controversial.

Therefore before the reforms contained in the Planning etc (Scotland) Act 2006 ('the 2006 Act') came into operation many of the planning applications for smaller scale developments, as well as the day-to-day operational decisions such as how a planning application should be dealt with, were matters for local authority officers exercising their powers under a scheme of delegation made under section 56(1) of the 1973 Act.

1973 Act schemes of delegation

The distinction between key decisions, particularly important policy decisions being taken by committee, and the day-to-day running of a local authority being carried out by decisions of officers, gives rise in most authorities to two main governance documents.

---

8 See Scottish Government Circular 1/2013: *Strategic Development Plan Areas* at www.gov.scot/Publications/2013/03/3286.

The first of these is a 'scheme of administration', which sets out what the remit of committees and sub-committees will be. The second is a 'scheme of delegation' or delegations, which gives specific powers to officers to carry out the functions of the council, including those relating to its function as planning authority.

A typical scheme of delegation under the 1973 Act will be relatively extensive, and delegate to officers a series of functions, usually along the lines of particular subject areas such as education, housing, environmental health and, of course, planning. The advent of the 2006 Act did not do away with the need for a 1973 Act scheme of delegation as regards planning matters. However, as discussed below, there is now a specific requirement for a scheme of delegation in relation to planning permission applications for 'local developments'.

Schemes of delegation under the 1973 Act will, of necessity, not describe every single decision an officer takes in the course of his or her working day.

The whole issue of just how specific a scheme of delegation has to be was considered in the case of *Uprichard v Fife Council*.[9] This case, which concerned Fife Council's decision to grant an application for planning permission for a hotel, golf course and leisure complex near St Andrews, had a number of issues. One was whether the council officers had power to decide whether or not an environmental statement was required before Fife Council decided to grant the application.

Lord Bonomy, applying *Dalziel School Board v The Scotch Education Department*,[10] took the view that 'the question is a mixed question of fact and law whether the power to make the decision was delegated to the officials who made it' and that given officers had the delegated authority to determine all non-controversial planning applications, they had delegated authority to 'take all decisions along the way in relation to such applications'.[11] He also said:

'A decision will be a valid decision where it is made at official level in accordance with an established practice of leaving such decisions

9 2000 SCLR 949.
10 1915 SC 234.
11 At para 36.

to officials, the particular official or officials varying according to the circumstances of the decision, where the decision is plainly one that could be delegated in terms of the Local Government (Scotland) Act 1973 and where it is consistent with the scheme of delegation made by the authority.'[12]

1997 Act schemes of delegation – 'local developments'

Section 43A(1) of the 1997 Act (Local developments: schemes of delegation) provides:

'A planning authority are—

(a) as soon as practicable after the coming into force of section 17 of the Planning etc (Scotland) Act 2006 (asp 17), and thereafter—

　　(i) whenever required to do so by the Scottish Ministers, or

　　(ii) subject to sub-paragraph (i), at such intervals as may be provided for in regulations under this section,

to prepare a scheme (to be known as a 'scheme of delegation') by which any application for planning permission for a development within the category of local developments or any application for consent, agreement or approval required by a condition imposed on a grant of planning permission for a development within that category is to be determined by a person appointed by them for the purposes of this section instead of by them, and

(b) to keep under review the scheme so prepared.'

The policy reasons behind the introduction of a specific scheme of delegation for planning matters have been discussed in Chapter 1. Essentially, there was a requirement to ensure that planning permission applications, particularly those of a relatively minor nature, are dealt with as quickly and efficiently as possible. Normally that would entail their determination being undertaken by a planning authority officer, rather than going through the planning authority's committee process.

There is nothing to stop the planning authority either preparing

---

12　At para 38.

a 1997 Act scheme of delegation which stands alone from the
remainder of any scheme of delegation made under the 1973 Act,
or incorporating a 1997 Act scheme of delegation into a 1973 Act
scheme of delegation. However, the 1997 Act delegation provisions need to be, at the very least, kept separate in the sense that it is
clear which parts of the overall scheme of delegation represent the
planning authority's scheme of delegation made under section
43A(1) of the 1997 Act.

Section 43A(2) of the 1997 Act provides that the determination
of a person appointed under a 1997 Act scheme of delegation shall
be treated as the planning authority's determination except for the
purposes of the provisions relating to the local review body (when
the appointed person's decision is presumably simply considered
to be that of the appointed officer as opposed to a decision on
behalf of the planning authority).

Section 43A(3) of the 1997 Act makes it clear that a local
review body cannot deal with an application requiring a pre-
determination hearing under section 38A of the 1997 Act. In other
words, any application for planning permission which needs a
pre-determination hearing cannot be determined by an appointed
officer or, in turn, a local review body.

Further statutory exceptions to what may be in a 1997 Act
scheme of delegation are set out at sections 43A(6) and 43A(7) of
the 1997 Act which, together, provide that a planning authority
may decide to determine an application which might otherwise fall
within a 1997 Act scheme of delegation, but that any such decision
that the application be determined by members (rather than
officers) of the authority, with the reason(s) therefor, must be
notified to the applicant.

The remaining provisions of section 43A of the 1997 Act which
are applicable to a 1997 Act scheme of delegation are:

- section 43A(4), which provides for regulations to give further
  detail; and
- section 43A(5), which applies other relevant parts of the
  1997 Act to any determination by a person appointed under a
  1997 Act scheme of delegation including section 37 of the 1997
  Act (determination of applications: general considerations).

Regulations made under section 43A of the 1997 Act

Section 43A(4) of the 1997 Act provides that regulations may make provision as to the form and content of and the procedures for preparing and adopting a 1997 Act scheme of delegation. The current regulations, which came into force on 30 June 2013, are the Town and Country Planning (Schemes of Delegation and Local Review Procedure) (Scotland) Regulations 2013 ('the 2013 Regulations').[13] Part 2 of the 2013 Regulations includes provisions about the content of a 1997 Act scheme of delegation.

Regulation 3(1) of the 2013 Regulations states that a scheme of delegation must describe the classes of development to which the scheme of delegation will apply. It must also state with respect to every such class which of the applications specified (the specified classes are applications for planning permission and applications for consent, agreement or approval required by a condition imposed on a grant of planning permission) are to be determined by an appointed officer. If such an application is only to be so determined in particular circumstances, the 1997 Act scheme of delegation must specify those circumstances.

It is worth noting that from 6 April 2009 until 29 June 2013 there was a requirement for any 1997 Act scheme of delegation to include a provision prohibiting an appointed officer from determining an application for planning permission where:

- the application was made by the planning authority; or a member of the planning authority; or

13 SSI 2013/157. These replaced earlier regulations, namely Town and Country Planning (Schemes of Delegation and Local Review Procedure) (Scotland) Regulations 2008 (SSI 2008/433 as amended by Town and Country Planning (Miscellaneous Amendments) (Scotland) Regulations 2009 (SSI 2009/220); Town and Country Planning (Miscellaneous Amendments) (Scotland) Regulations 2011 (SSI 2011/138) and Town and Country Planning (Miscellaneous Amendments) (Scotland) Regulations 2012 (SSI 2012/325). The 2013 Regulations also revoke reg 5 of Town and Country Planning (Miscellaneous Amendments) (Scotland) Regulations 2009 (SSI 2009/220) and reg 4 of Town and Country Planning (Miscellaneous Amendments) (Scotland) Regulations 2011 (SSI 2011/138).

- the application related to land in the ownership of the planning authority or to land in which the planning authority has a financial interest.[14]

This requirement to specify that prohibition is not included in the 2013 Regulations. However, this does not mean that authorities must delegate power to their officers to determine those planning authority interest cases.

Therefore, subject to the provisions of the relevant 1997 Act scheme of delegation, it is now possible that an application by the planning authority itself or a member of that authority or an application relating to land in which the planning authority has an ownership or financial interest could be determined by an appointed officer and thereafter be dealt with by a local review body. In other words, decisions on such applications might only be challenged outwith the planning authority on the basis of a challenge to the legality of the decision to grant the application by a person applying to the Court of Session.

Further, it is also worth noting that although the wording of regulation 3 of the 2013 Regulations is quite general in its reference to 'applications for planning permission', section 43A of the 1997 Act specifically states that the scheme of delegation only relates to applications for planning permission for 'local developments'. In most cases, planning authorities will want applications for planning permission for 'major developments' to be dealt with by committee. However, should they wish to delegate any of them, it would be sensible to deal with provisions relating to that in a part of any scheme of delegation separate from the part dealing with any scheme of delegation in relation to planning applications for 'local developments'.

Regulation 4 of the 2013 Regulations provides that where a planning authority proposes to adopt a scheme of delegation, the authority must send a copy of the scheme of delegation to the Scottish Ministers, and the planning authority must not adopt the

---

14 Town and Country Planning (Schemes of Delegation and Local Review Procedure) (Scotland) Regulations 2008 (SSI 2008/433), regs 3(3) and 3(4).

scheme of delegation until it has been approved by the Scottish Ministers. This requirement should be followed by planning authorities and a record kept of approval to any changes in the scheme of delegation.

Regulation 5 of the 2013 Regulations includes provisions about publication of a 1997 Act scheme of delegation, and provides that a planning authority must make a copy of the adopted 1997 Act scheme of delegation available for inspection at an office of the planning authority and in every public library in the planning authority's area, as well as publishing the adopted scheme of delegation on the internet.

Regulation 6 of the 2013 Regulations provides for the planning authority to prepare a 1997 Act scheme of delegation at intervals of no greater than every five years. In practice, it is likely that any planning authority will wish to review how the scheme of delegation is operating at shorter intervals than that. However, this at least allows for the scheme of delegation to be reviewed formally, and adopted, once every council term.

The statutory requirements for a scheme of delegation are therefore relatively brief. This is in line with the policy that the regulations should be 'light touch', and allow for local variations. In practice, each scheme of delegation in the 33 planning authorities (the 32 local authorities and the Loch Lomond and The Trossachs National Park Authority) is slightly different, although there are similarities.

Local variations

Planning authorities should have regard, in drafting or amending their 1997 Act scheme of delegation, to the Scottish Government's Circular 5/2013: *Schemes of Delegation and Local Reviews.*[15] As regards schemes of delegation, the circular largely confines itself to outlining the relevant legislative provisions. However, it does state:

15 www.gov.scot/Publications/2013/12/8902

'The Government's view is that there should be flexibility to enable planning authorities to develop clear schemes of delegation appropriate to local circumstances.'[16]

Key local variations to 1997 Act schemes of delegation will relate to when a 'local development' application must be considered by committee. Shortly after the provisions of the 2006 Act came into force, a review was carried out of the schemes of delegation made under section 43A of the 1997 Act and the then extant regulations. Not surprisingly, there were significant variations between the classes of development which planning authorities wished to except from delegated decision by appointed officer, although there were similarities and common themes.[17]

It is worth remembering at this stage what might constitute a 'local development'. The regulations made under section 26A(2) of the 1997 Act provide that 'local developments' are all developments other than 'national developments' (that is development or classes of development designated as such in the National Planning Framework under section 3A(4)(b) of the 1997 Act) and 'major developments' (currently defined in the Town and Country Planning (Hierarchy of Developments) (Scotland) Regulations 2009 – see Chapter 1).[18] It is possible by means of reference to the schedule in those 2009 Regulations, to be relatively clear what would normally constitute a 'local development'.

The most common categories of 'local development' therefore are:

- housing where the development comprises 49 or fewer proposed homes and the area of the site is less than 2 hectares (so, for instance, a proposed development of 40 houses on a 2-hectare site would not be a 'local development' because although the number of homes is 49 or fewer the site area is not less than 2 hectares);
- construction of a building, structure or other erection for use for any of the following purposes: (a) office; (b) research and

16 At para 13.
17 www.brodies.com/node/1366
18 Town and Country Planning (Hierarchy of Developments) (Scotland) Regulations 2009 (SSI 2009/51), reg 2(2).

development of products or processes; (c) any industrial process; or (d) use for storage or as a distribution centre, where
the gross floor space of the building structure or other erection
is less than 10,000 square metres and the area of the site is less
than 2 hectares;

- construction of facilities for use for the purpose of waste
  management or disposal where the capacity of the facility is
  less than 25,000 tonnes per annum or in relation to facilities
  for use for the purpose of sludge treatment with a capacity to
  treat a maximum of 50 tonnes (wet weight) per day of
  residual sludge;
- construction of new replacement roads, railways, tramways,
  waterways, aqueducts or pipelines where the maximum
  length is 8 kilometres;
- placing or assembly of equipment for the purpose of fish
  farming within the meaning of section 26(6) of the 1997 Act
  where the surface area of water covered is less than 2
  hectares;
- extraction of minerals where the area of the site is less than 2
  hectares; and
- any development not falling wholly within any single class
  of development described in the above categories where the
  gross floor space of any building, structure or erection constructed as a result of such development is less than 5,000
  square metres and the area of the site is less than 2 hectares.

Schemes of delegation may make specific reference to all or any
of these categories or sub-classes of development, such as wind
farms or telecommunication masts which are to be excluded from
the operation of delegated powers. Other common exceptions are
listed below. That list of exceptions is not exhaustive.

Planning authority interest developments

Prior to 30 June 2013 the most common exception from delegation
was planning authority 'local development' applications and applications for 'local development' of land which was either within the
planning authority's ownership or in which the planning authority
had a financial interest.

As noted above, since 30 June 2013 there has been no legislative requirement to prohibit an appointed officer being empowered to determine 'local development' applications made by the planning authority or one of its members or which relates to land in the ownership of the planning authority or in which the planning authority has a financial interest. However, some planning authorities may still wish to continue to except such instances from delegation to an appointed officer. Further, some schemes of delegation expand the category of local authority interest applications to include, for example, applications made by partners, close friends or relatives of planning authority members and/or officers involved in the statutory planning process and their partners, close friends or relatives.

Representations – of opposition or support

The next most common exception from delegation to an appointed officer is where a number of representations has been received. The exception may relate to the number of objections, or may contain further qualifications about whether the representations raise specific material planning issues. Some schemes of delegation may relate this exception only to objections, whereas others will also include a trigger level where a number of representations in support of an application will mean that the application is not dealt with under delegated powers.

The identity of objectors may also be significant: planning authorities may wish to decide at committee any applications which have attracted objections from community councils either acting as statutory objectors or otherwise or, more generally, any statutory objectors.

Decision by planning authority as opposed to its appointed officer

A more general provision will often allow the planning authority to decide itself to determine the application in terms of section 43A(6) of the 1997 Act. The power to decide to refer the matter to committee may itself be delegated. The scheme of delegation may go on to set out circumstances in which this power may be used. Any decision made under this would require to include a statement of the reasons for the decision which should be served on the applicant.[19]

Member referral

What is considered by some to be the most controversial exception to a scheme of delegation is where a member has requested that an application be referred to committee rather than dealt with under delegated powers. This was a very common exception to delegation under schemes of delegation in operation prior to the introduction of the current system from 3 August 2009. However, effectively giving an individual member (or even more than one member, outwith committee) a power of referral is questionable given the wording of section 56 of the 1973 Act. Provisions of this nature, however, do appear to have been approved by the Scottish Ministers in current 1997 Act schemes of delegation.

Environmental impact assessment

Some schemes of delegation exclude from delegation any applications which require an environmental impact assessment. The thinking behind this is that such applications tend to be of a complexity which would be difficult to consider fully in the context of a local review body.

Proposed development contrary to the development plan

Schemes of delegation may also except from delegation applications for 'local development' which are contrary to the development plan. This may be further qualified to only those applications which the appointed officer is minded to approve.

Associated applications

Planning authorities may consider it prudent to exclude from the operation of delegated powers any applications which have associated applications such as listed building consent. The reason for this

19 1997 Act, s 43A(7).

is that should both applications be refused, the planning application will fall to be determined by the local review body while the listed building consent will be determined by the Scottish Ministers (in practice normally the Scottish Government's Directorate for Planning and Environmental Appeals ('DPEA')).

It may be considered to be unfair to the applicant to require them to use two completely distinct planning processes where the applications have basically been for the same development. It is also likely to increase delay and the possibility of conflicting decisions being taken by the DPEA and the local review body.

Disputes about schemes of delegation

The introduction of 1997 Act schemes of delegation for 'local developments' has complicated, rather than simplified, the planning landscape.[20] These complications may lead to a council's Monitoring Officer being called upon to resolve whether an officer can properly determine a planning permission application under a scheme of delegation.[21]

20 'Delegation procedures: a tool for simplified planning?' (2009) 136 SPEL 135.
21 See Chapter 9.

Chapter 3

Local Planning Reviews: Governance and General Approach to Decision-making

Chapter 1 provides an introduction to the background and concept of local planning reviews in Scotland. Chapter 2 addresses the requirements for schemes of delegation made under section 43A of the 1997 Act empowering appointed planning authority officers to determine most, though not all, 'local development' planning applications.

As shall be seen in this chapter:

- any local review body established under section 43A of the 1997 Act by a planning authority to review 'local development' planning applications (including the failure to determine such an application within the prescribed period or the period agreed between the applicant and the appointed officer – which is deemed to be a refusal of the application) must be a committee of the planning authority;
- the provisions of the Ethical Standards in Public Life etc (Scotland) Act 2000 and related codes of conduct are relevant; and
- there has been a lack of certainty about the approach that a local review body should adopt in undertaking a review (a review of the appointed officer's decision or consideration of the planning application as if it had been made to the local review body in the first instance) and about what matters may be raised in a review under section 43A(8) of the 1997 Act.

Local review body must be a committee of the planning authority

Regulation 7(1) of the Town and Country Planning (Schemes of Delegation and Local Review Procedure) (Scotland) Regulations 2013 ('the 2013 Regulations') states:

> 'A review of a case by virtue of section 43A(8) of the [1997] Act is to be conducted by a committee of the planning authority comprising at least three members of the authority (to be known as the "local review body").'

The Local Government (Scotland) Act 1973 ('the 1973 Act') empowers a local authority, in terms of section 56, to arrange for the discharge of any of its functions by a committee, a sub-committee, an officer of the authority or by any other local authority in Scotland. The interaction of that section and regulation 7 of the 2013 Regulations indicates that the functions of a review require to be carried out by a committee, rather than by either an officer or a sub-committee of the planning authority.

This is not to say that initial administrative arrangements and even initial procedural decisions relating to how and when to hold meetings of a review body cannot be carried out by planning authority officers. However, the substantive decisions of a local review body are to be taken by a committee of the planning authority. This does have some implications for the way in which a local planning review decision in Scotland can be taken in terms of process.

Establishing the local review body

The first point is that the planning authority, in setting up its local review body, should have provided for its existence in its scheme of administration, the governance document which sets out the system of committees and sub-committees by which the local authority intends to discharge some of its functions under section 56 of the 1973 Act (in other words, those functions which are not to be discharged by the council itself, by its officers under the scheme of delegation or otherwise by means of joint committees or other local authorities).

Section 57(2) of the 1973 Act makes it clear that the number of members of a committee, their term of office and the area (if restricted) within which the committee is to exercise its authority, are to be fixed by the council itself.[1]

Section 57(3) of the 1973 Act also provides that a committee may include persons who are not councillors, but at least two thirds of the members appointed should be. This does, in fact, give planning authorities the ability to appoint non-elected members to the local review body, although this does not appear to have happened anywhere in Scotland so far. However, given the requirement in regulation 7 of the 2013 Regulations that the review is to be conducted by a 'committee comprising at least three members of the authority', it is suggested that non-councillor members of the review body could only sit on any review body in addition to three elected members. However, the appointment of non-elected members would not sit well with the position success-fully advocated by some local authorities about the need for decision-taking by democratically elected members.

It is perfectly possible and has, indeed, become usual practice for the overall committee, which forms the local review body, to be a larger number than simply the basic minimum of three elected members, even though any meeting of the local review body itself may not comprise the entire committee. This enables officers administering the local review body to relieve the pressure on elected members' time by not asking them to attend every local review body meeting. However, there is a concomitant need to ensure that the scheme of administration properly sets out what constitutes a quorum of each meeting. Standing regulation 7(1) of the 2013 Regulations, that quorum could not be less than three elected members.

Access to local planning review meeting, publication of documents etc

So far as other legislative requirements relating to membership of committees are concerned, the usual provisions relating to disquali-

---

1 Local Government (Scotland) Act 1973 ('1973 Act'), s 57(2).

fication for membership of committees apply.[2] Perhaps more importantly, the provisions of sections 50A–50K of the 1973 Act relating to access to meetings and documents of local authorities and, in particular, the requirements for agendas and associated papers to be available for public inspection at least three clear days before the meeting, will also apply to meetings of the local review body.[3]

Section 50B of the 1973 Act, which has minimum requirements regarding access to reports as well as the agenda, should be interpreted to include notices of review and related documentation. This is separate from the requirement under regulation 11 of the 2013 Regulations that the review documents are to be made available for inspection at an office of the planning authority until such time as the review is determined. Similarly, the requirements for inspection of minutes[4] and background papers[5] should be borne in mind.

Another implication for local review bodies arising from the statutory provisions on committees relates to Schedule 7 of the 1973 Act. Paragraph 7(1) of that schedule (which is applied to committees by virtue of paragraph 10 of that schedule) states that minutes of a committee meeting shall be drawn up and shall be signed at the same or the next following meeting by the person presiding and any minute purporting to be so signed shall be received in evidence without further proof.

This imposes on the local review body a requirement to produce a minute of the meeting which is separate from the requirement to issue a decision notice under regulation 22 of the 2013 Regulations. It is good practice to issue a brief minute relating to the steps in procedure carried out by the local review body at its meeting,

---

2 1973 Act, s 59.

3 Failure to make relevant papers available to the public at the requisite time may lead to the decision being quashed unless the authority can demonstrate that the authority would inevitably have come to the same conclusion even if the information had been available. The probability that the decision would have been the same is not enough. See, for instance, *R (on the application of Joicey) v Northumberland County Council* [2014] EWHC 3657 (Admin).

4 1973 Act, s 50C.

5 1973 Act, s 50D.

and the basic outcome of the review (to uphold, reverse or vary the determination (including deemed refusal) reviewed). The content of the local review body's decision, and the reason(s) for arriving at it, must be set out in the decision notice required by regulation 22 of the 2013 Regulations. The content of the decision notice of the local review body is addressed in Chapter 8.

It is also worth noting that minutes of the local review body will require to be presented again to the following meeting in normal course, when the members of the local review body might well be different. However, the planning authority should ensure that, at the very least, one of the officers present at the next meeting can vouch for the accuracy of the minutes. Paragraph 10(2) of Schedule 7 to the 1973 Act makes it clear that any minute made and signed in accordance with paragraph 7 constitutes prima facie proof of the local review body having been duly constituted, having had power to deal with the matters referred to in the minute, the meeting being deemed to have been duly convened and held, and the members present having been deemed to have been duly qualified to deal with the relevant business.

A further consequence of the local review body being a committee of a local authority is that normally it will be subject to the same standing orders as other committee meetings. Section 62 of the 1973 Act enables a local authority to make standing orders regulating the procedure to be followed at its meetings including those of its committees. Standing orders generally deal with such matters as procedures to be followed by the Chair of the committee, the general conduct of business, debate, formal motions made, voting and the general decision-making powers of committees. Such standing orders are reviewed on a regular basis, as they constitute the primary rules by which committees conduct their proceedings. Indeed, there is English case law indicating that once a local authority has made standing orders it is obliged to follow them in its meetings – unless the authority is following approved means for temporarily suspending standing orders which are often written into the orders themselves.[6]

---

6 See D Upton & S Taylor, *Knowles on Local Authority Meetings: A Manual of Law and Practice* (6th edn) and the cases discussed in paras 2.12ff.

In reviewing the standing orders, planning authorities should ensure that there is nothing in them that is inappropriate for the specialised nature of a local review body meeting.

Standing orders will often set out the requirements for an agenda for any committee meeting. A local review body meeting therefore may have an agenda that will partly comply with the legislative requirements and partly be in line with standing orders and will comprise the following:

- name of authority;
- date, place and time of meeting;
- apologies;
- declarations of interest;
- minute of last meeting; and
- the substantive cases to be considered at that meeting of the local review body.

Although the law relating to how a committee should act is relatively brief, those organising a local review body should be aware of any interactions between that law, the planning authority's standing orders and the requirements of the planning legislation which establishes local review bodies.

For example, many standing orders will provide for urgent business to be transacted at a committee meeting, something provided for in paragraph 2(4) of Schedule 7 to the 1973 Act. However, given the nature of the matters being discussed at a local review body, it would not be appropriate to bring forward review cases which had not been circulated at least three clear days in advance and of which the public – particularly the applicant – had no notice.

Similarly, the well-known provisions in the 1973 Act about exclusion of the press and public[7] are contrary to other requirements such as the provision in the 2013 Regulations that all meetings of a local review body at which decisions will be made about the further review procedure (written submissions, hearing session(s), site inspection or a combination of any of these pro-

---

7 1973 Act, s 50A.

cedures), or how the case under review is to be determined, must be held in public.[8]

The Councillors' Code of Conduct

The elected members of a local authority who sit on a local review body are bound by the Councillors' Code of Conduct ('the Code') in local review body matters as much as in all their other activities.

The Code will be familiar to all elected members of councils. It was first introduced by the Ethical Standards in Public Life etc (Scotland) Act 2000 ('the 2000 Act') and its current iteration was approved by the Scottish Parliament and came into effect on 21 December 2010.[9]

Other public bodies, such as the Loch Lomond and The Trossachs National Park Authority which has a local review body, have their own bespoke Code of Conduct.[10]

The Standards Commission for Scotland ('the Standards Commission'), the body which enforces the provisions of the Code, has also published guidance about the Code.

Complaints and sanctions

Complaints against councillors under the Code are made initially to the Commissioner for Ethical Standards in Public Life in Scotland who will investigate them and decide whether to make a report to the Standards Commission.[11] Although cases which the Commissioner considers to be serious enough to warrant being reported to the Standards Commission are relatively rare,[12] the sanctions which can be applied by the Standards Commission for breach of the Code under section 19 of the 2000 Act are potentially

8 2013 Regulations, reg 7(2).
9 www.gov.scot/Publications/2010/12/10145144/0
10 www.standardscommissionscotland.org.uk/content/which-bodies-have-codes
11 www.ethicalstandards.org.uk/
12 www.standardscommissionscotland.org.uk/full.list

serious. Therefore observing the Code is not taken lightly by either councillors or officers advising them.

The sanctions which can be applied for breach of the Code are:

- censure;
- suspension, for a period not exceeding one year, of the councillor's entitlement to attend one or more but not all of the following: all meetings of the council; all meetings of one or more committees or sub-committees; or all meetings of any other body on which that councillor is a representative or nominee of the council;
- suspension, for a period not exceeding one year, of the councillor's entitlement to attend all meetings of the council and of any committee or sub-committee of the council; and of any other body on which the councillor is a representative or nominee of the council; and
- disqualifying the councillor, for a period not exceeding five years, from being or being nominated for election as, or from being elected as, a councillor.

Any period of suspension would come to an end at any ordinary election. Disqualification has the effect of vacating the councillor's office and extends to the membership of any joint committees, joint boards and so on.[13]

Should any non-councillor members be added to a local review body, it is likely that they would be expected to observe the terms of the Code, although it is not entirely clear how any breaches by them would be enforced.

Provisions of the Code

The Code is set out in seven sections. The first three sections introduce the Code and its key principles and deal with general conduct. Section 4 of the Code introduces a requirement for members to note, on a register kept by the council, any interests that members consider are significant enough to potentially affect their ability to

13 Annex A to the Code of Conduct.

take decisions at council or in committee. These interests can be financial (for example, ownership of land or buildings or other employment) or non-financial (most commonly membership of other organisations or relationships with particular people which might affect the councillor's ability to be seen to be taking a decision impartially).

Section 5 of the Code addresses declarations of interest at meetings. In some situations, elected members may be entitled to declare a non-financial interest but remain at the meeting. However, as set out below, this is not the case at local review bodies.

Section 6 of the Code deals with lobbying and access to councillors. It states that councillors should expect to be lobbied, but need to make clear to those lobbying them that they are not in a position to indicate support or otherwise for particular proposals, particularly in matters such as planning.

Paragraph 6.3 of the Code states:

'You may be lobbied by a wide range of people including individuals, organisations, companies and developers. As a general rule, it is an essential element of the democratic system that any individual should be able to lobby the council or a councillor. However, particular considerations apply when you are dealing with applications under regulatory powers such as planning and matters of a quasi-judicial nature such as the determination of certain licence applications. If you are lobbied on such matters, you should make it clear that you are not in a position to lend support for or against any such application that you will have responsibility for making a decision on in due course. Representations to councillors on such applications should be directed, by the councillor, to the appropriate department of the council. This does not prevent you from seeking factual information about the progress of the case.'

Section 7 of the Code is devoted to situations where councillors take decisions on quasi-judicial or regulatory applications. Paragraph 7.3 makes it clear that, independently of the legal obligation for decision-makers to act without bias and without having closed their mind in advance of the decision-making process, councillors must not only act fairly but also be seen to be acting fairly; they must not pre-judge or demonstrate bias, or be seen to be prejudging or demonstrating bias, in respect of any decision taken at a relevant meeting.

Paragraph 7.5 of the Code makes it clear that the exclusions which apply in respect of declarations of interests for appointments to outside bodies in section 5 of the Code do not apply in relation to any matter of a quasi-judicial or regulatory nature. Accordingly, where the applicant for review is a body to which the elected member has been appointed (or is an interested party), he or she should declare an interest and withdraw from any consideration in the local review body.

Paragraph 7.9 of the Code specifically mentions local review body membership as one of the areas where councillors may have to deal with planning decisions. That being the case, it is clear that members of a local review body are bound by the remaining provisions of section 7 of the Code and, in particular, the following provisions need to be considered:

- Local review body members should never seek to pressure planning officers to provide a particular recommendation or seek privately to lobby other councillors who have a responsibility for dealing with the application in question – the latter also being relevant for councillors even when they are not sitting on a particular local review body (paragraph 7.10).
- Councillors should not give any grounds to question their impartiality and should be very careful not to make any public statement which indicates or implies support or opposition to a particular proposed development or to declare any voting intention before any relevant meeting (paragraph 7.11).
- If a local review body member has an interest, whether financial or non-financial, in the outcome of a decision at the local review body, they should declare that interest and not take part in making the decision (paragraph 7.12).
- Local review body members should not organise support for or opposition to or lobby other councillors or act as an advocate to promote a particular outcome on a review by the local review body (paragraph 7.13).
- Councillors should follow any guidance on site visits provided by the planning authority (paragraph 7.23) and consider the

guidance about site inspections published by the Local Review Body Forum.[14] The purpose of a site visit is to allow the members of the local review body to become familiar with the physical aspects of the application site and the surrounding area. The guidance will normally recommend that members on a site inspection do not engage with the applicant or other parties in the course of the inspection regarding the merits of the proposed development and that they confine any engagement to asking whether any person wants to draw attention to physical factors in relation to the proposed development.

Paragraphs 7.14 and 7.15 of the Code address representations about planning applications. While, as noted above, paragraph 7.13 makes it clear that a councillor should not organise support for or opposition to or lobby other councillors or act as an advocate to promote a particular recommendation, paragraph 7.14 softens this line slightly by stating that a councillor is not precluded from 'raising issues or concerns on any of the matters associated with the application with the planning officers concerned'.

While this is entirely correct in terms of a planning application which is to come before a planning committee, it is suggested that in the context of the heightened concerns over fairness and the impartiality of a local review body, it would not be appropriate for a councillor to contact either the appointed officer who made the decision or, indeed, the local review body's planning adviser, out-with a local review body meeting to make known any representations from constituents or applicants, even if the councillor were then to declare their interest at the review body and withdraw in terms of paragraph 7.15 of the Code.

On one view, planning authority officers making arrangements for meetings of local review bodies may well wish to avoid difficulties relating to the Code by ensuring that any councillors considering a particular application for review are not ward councillors for the area in which the proposed development is located. However, another view is that this would be inconsistent with the objective of increased local accountability.

14 www.gov.scot/Resource/0038/00389406.pdf

Review of the appointed officer's decision and matters which may be raised in a review

As planning authorities sought to put together governance structures for local planning reviews, a fundamental question arose. In reviewing the appointed officer's decision, was the planning authority acting through its local review body:

- considering the planning application before it as if the application had been made to it in the first instance;[15] or
- reviewing the appointed officer's decision to see whether it is 'appropriate'?[16]

Further, could a local review body consider any matter that was not raised, or documents, materials or evidence that were not provided, before the appointed officer decided the 'local development' planning application?

The lack of clarity around these issues is considered in the remainder of this chapter.

2005 Scottish Executive White Paper: Modernising the Planning System

The Scottish Executive's 2005 White Paper *Modernising the Planning System*[17] includes the following statements about local planning reviews in Scotland:

'Applicants will have the right to appeal to a local review body against decisions taken by planning authority officers [regarding planning applications for 'local developments']. The review body will be made up of locally elected members. The applicant will submit grounds of appeal, which will be supplied to the [local] review body accompanied by the case file, a copy of the [appointed] officer's decision and his or her response to the grounds

---

15 Often referred to as 'the *de novo* approach'.

16 See Scottish Government 2008 consultation paper *Modernising Planning Appeals* below. See also Scottish Government Circular 6/2013: *Development Planning* which indicates, at para 117, that the test to be applied by the Scottish Ministers' reporters in considering the proposed plan is one of 'appropriateness and sufficiency' and not one of 'soundness'.

17 www.gov.scot/Resource/Doc/54357/0014194.pdf

for appeal. The review body will then carry out an independent review of the officer's decision, rather than considering the proposal afresh. The review body's decision could be the subject of a statutory appeal or judicial review. These measures, taken together, would result in a significant improvement to the planning process at the local level. A key benefit would be that the vast majority of all appeals would henceforth be decided quickly and decided locally, recognising that local authorities are best placed to take decisions on local matters.[18]

'From now on, all planning appeals will revert to being a review of the decision made by the planning authority, based on the material that was supplied to the planning authority by the applicant and the representations made to them by the community. Only in exceptional circumstances, such as a change in national or development plan policy, will consideration extend beyond the matters contained in the planning application as considered by the planning authority and explained to the community.'[19]

Therefore the 2005 White Paper indicated that:

- a local review body would carry out a review of the appointed officer's decision (including deemed refusal of the planning application) and would not consider any planning application for 'local development' 'afresh' (ie as if it had been made to it in the first instance);[20] and
- a local review body would only be able in 'exceptional circumstances' to consider matters which had not been contained in the relevant 'local development' planning permission application determined (including any deemed refusal) by the planning authority's appointed officer.

Planning etc (Scotland) Act 2006 and the 1997 Act

The Planning etc (Scotland) Act 2006 inserted into the 1997 Act

---

18 At para 5.1.4.
19 At para 5.3.3.
20 1997 Act, s 48 refers to a planning permission appeal being considered as if the relevant planning application had been made to the Scottish Ministers in the first instance – that is that it could be considered 'afresh' or '*de novo*'.

section 43A, subsection (8)[21] of which states:

'Where [an appointed officer]—

    (a) refuses an application for planning permission or for consent, agreement or approval,

    (b) grants it subject to conditions, or

    (c) has not determined it within such period as may be prescribed by regulations or a development order or within such extended period as may at any time be agreed upon in writing between the applicant and the person so appointed,

the applicant may require the planning authority to review the case.'

Section 43A(10) of the 1997 Act provides that regulations or a development order may make provision as to the 'form and procedures of any review conducted by virtue of subsection (8)'. Subsections (11) to (14) then set out certain requirements as regards the regulations. Subsection (15) states that the planning authority (acting through its local review body) 'may uphold, reverse or vary a determination reviewed by them by virtue of subsection (8)'.

The Planning etc (Scotland) Act 2006 inserted into the 1997 Act section 43B which states:

'(1) In a review under section 43A(8), a party to the proceedings is not to raise any matter which was not before the appointed person at the time the determination reviewed was made unless that party can demonstrate—

    (a) that the matter could not have been raised before that time, or

    (b) that its not being raised before that time was a consequence of exceptional circumstances.

(2) Nothing in subsection (1) affects any requirement or entitlement to have regard to—

    (a) the provisions of the development plan; or

    (b) any other material consideration.'

---

21 As amended by Public Services Reform (Planning) (Local Review Procedure) (Scotland) Order 2013 (SSI 2013/24).

Section 43B of the 1997 Act is in substantially the same terms as section 47A of the 1997 Act (matters which may be raised in an appeal under section 47(1)). The policy objective of those provisions was, in general, to prohibit new issues being raised after the planning authority's decision.[22] In his evidence to the Scottish Parliament about matters which may be raised in appeals the Scottish Executive Chief Reporter said '[t]he objective is to increase the certainty for communities that are engaging with the process and to stop drift and the stress that is caused by drift' and that '[t]here is no intention to embargo additional material that is material and relevant to the outcome.'[23]

2008 Scottish Government consultation paper *Modernising Planning Appeals*

The Scottish Government's 2008 consultation paper *Modernising Planning Appeals*,[24] which included draft Local Review Procedure regulations, includes the following statements:

'[The introduction of making the review of local developments the responsibility of planning authorities rather than that of the Scottish Ministers] must not result in a reduction in the quality of examination, one of the key strengths of the existing [planning permission appeals] system. It is essential that any local review process is underpinned by high standards: those with responsibility for participating as members or chairing a local review body must be fully trained; there must be clear timescales for requiring and responding to reviews; those requesting a review must be confident that their case will be dealt with fairly; clear reasons explaining the decision of the review body must be made available and, crucially, the local review body must operate in a way that demonstrates independence from the original decision-taker. Some of

22 See, for instance, Planning etc (Scotland) Bill, Policy Memorandum at para 162.

23 Jim McCulloch, Chief Reporter, Communities Committee, 8 February 2006, columns 3026 and 3027.

24 www.gov.scot/Resource/Doc/212344/0056504.pdf

these issues will be best dealt with in guidance rather than regulations.[25]

'[T]he applicant should explain, where new issues have been raised, why these could not have been raised earlier in the process or what exceptional circumstances apply to support their introduction. This is consistent with the provisions to focus on the material before the planning authority at the point when the delegated decision was taken.[26]

'The review process will focus on the material which was before the planning authority and consider whether the decision taken under delegated powers was appropriate. The review body may uphold, reverse or vary the decision. Where the requirement to review follows non-determination (a deemed refusal), the review body will be able to take a decision on the proposal. In cases of non-determination it will be necessary for advice on the planning merits of the case to be provided to the review body and for such material to be made available for comment to the applicant.[27]

'The review process is not intended to be adversarial. The review body will take into account the material before the planning authority during the planning process, including any report of handling, together with the supporting material lodged by the applicant in seeking a review. . . . [A]ny new issues not raised in the decision notice which are to be relied upon will be notified to the applicant and for him/her to comment on these . . . before the case is considered. Where, exceptionally, new material has been introduced into the process at review stage, parties to the review will be given an opportunity to comment on that material.'[28]

The 2008 consultation paper indicates that any local review body would consider whether the appointed officer's decision was 'appropriate' and envisaged that new issues and new materials could be taken into account by any local review body before reaching its decision.

---

25 At para 21.
26 At para 22.
27 At para 25.
28 At para 27.

Review of the appointed officer's decision?

A 'review' suggests to many a different process from that of an 'appeal'. The former suggests a more limited form of reassessment than an 'appeal' which suggests a full reassessment of the matter under consideration. Section 43A(15) of the 1997 Act refers to the planning authority upholding, reversing or varying the determination reviewed by it.

The approach of reviewing an original decision is not without precedent in local authority procedures. For example, many authorities have a sub-committee to deal with appeals against dismissal of employees. It is common for the remit of such a sub-committee to make it clear that the members are not entitled to rehear the substance of the case, but are instead to look at the process by which the employee was dismissed and determine whether it was properly followed to the extent that the employee should not be reinstated.

There are a number of reasons why it might be thought that the intention of the relevant legislation is to empower a planning authority to review the appointed officer's decision as opposed to empowering the planning authority (acting through its local review body) to consider the planning application before it as if the application had been made to it in the first instance.

As noted above, the government's 2005 White Paper specifically states that the local review body will carry out a review of the officer's decision 'rather than considering the proposal afresh'. Further the Scottish Government's 2008 consultation paper refers to a local review body considering whether the appointed officer's decision was 'appropriate'.

Although much of the wording in section 43A of the 1997 Act and the related regulations mirrors that of provisions regarding planning appeals the wording is not completely consistent. Most markedly, section 48(1) of the 1997 Act provides:

'on an appeal under section 47, the Secretary of State may—
    (a) allow or dismiss the appeal, or
    (b) reverse or vary any part of the decision of the planning
        authority (whether the appeal relates to that part of it or
        not),

and may deal with the application as if it had been made to him in the first instance.'

Review of the 'local development' planning application afresh?

In July 2011, almost two years after local review bodies were established, the Scottish Government's Chief Planner issued a letter on the issue of whether reviews by local review bodies 'should be conducted by means of a full consideration of the application afresh (*de novo*), or whether they are solely a review of the appointed officer's decision'. That letter set out the Scottish Government's position that the '*de novo*' approach should be adopted in determining cases brought before local review bodies. The Annex to the letter includes the following points:

- Although termed a 'review' the decision of a local review body was still the decision of the planning authority on a planning application and the same considerations would apply to the factors that require to be taken into account when making a decision in the first instance on such an application.

- Section 43A(5) made it clear that requirements to have regard to the development plan and any other material considerations remained in place, a point underlined separately in section 43B(2).

- Although section 43A did not contain the same wording as section 48(1) about the Scottish Ministers, when dealing with appeals, being able to deal with the application as if it had been made to them in the first instance, this was deemed not necessary in the case of a local review body determination because the application was made to, and was being determined by, the planning authority.

- The powers to reverse, vary or uphold the determination made by a planning officer available to a local review body mirrored the powers of Scottish Ministers on appeal.

In concluding, the Scottish Government's Chief Planner stressed the importance of planning authorities dealing with local review body cases consistently.[29]

---

29 www.gov.scot/Resource/0042/00427362.pdf

The Scottish Government's December 2013 Circular 5/2013: *Schemes of Delegation and Local Reviews* does not refer to, or supersede, the Chief Planner's July 2011 letter.[30]

Judicial consideration of local review body decision-making

The case of *Carroll v Scottish Borders Council* concerned the grant, by a review body, of planning permission for a wind farm which Mrs Carroll, an objector, claimed was contrary to the planning authority's policies.[31]

In his January 2014 decision Lord Armstrong said:

'It is significant that what is to be carried out is a review and not an appeal. In contrast to an appeal to the Scottish Ministers under section 47, there is no provision to the effect that the application is to be dealt with by the [local review body] as if it had been made in the first instance.'[32]

Matters that may be raised in a review under section 43A(8) of the 1997 Act

Section 43B(1) of the 1997 Act provides that, save in specified circumstances

'In a review under section 43A(8) [of the 1997 Act] a party to the proceedings is not to raise any matter which was not before the appointed person at the time the determination reviewed was made. . .'.

It is worth noting that:

- the phrase 'a party to the proceedings' is not just relevant to the applicant but to any party, whether a person who has made representations in relation to the 'local development' planning permission application, or a person required to make written submissions; and

---

30 www.gov.scot/Publications/2013/12/8902
31 [2014] CSOH 6.
32 At para 44.

- it is any 'matter' which was not before the appointed person at the time the determination reviewed was made that is not to be raised in a review.

'Matter' is not defined in the relevant legislation. The 2013 Regulations differentiate between 'matters' and 'documents', 'material' and 'evidence'. It appears that 'matter' must be interpreted as any issue or topic, and that the legislation excludes raising any new issue or topic that had not been raised as part of the application for 'local development' permission etc which was determined by the appointed officer. This interpretation is consistent with the interpretation adopted in relation to the equivalent provision in the appeals process by the Scottish Government's Directorate for Planning and Environmental Appeals ('DPEA') in its *Reporters Guidance Note 16 – New Matters and the submission of documents, material or evidence* about section 47A of the 1997 Act (matters which may be raised in an appeal under section 47(1)).[33]

However, even if the 'matter' is not raised by any party to the proceedings then, standing the terms of section 25 of the 1997 Act, a local review body will be required to consider a 'matter' that was not raised before the decision on the 'local development' application was taken by the appointed officer (see below).

Comments about uncertainties in local review body decision-making

Much of the uncertainty regarding the approach that a local review body should adopt, and what matters may be raised in a review under section 43A(8) of the 1997 Act, is caused by the inconsistencies between statements in the 2005 White Paper, the 2008 consultation paper *Modernising Planning Appeals* and the relevant legislation, the inconsistencies in expressions used in articulating matters and the tensions between the relevant primary and secondary legislation. For instance, if the DPEA appeals process was to

33 www.gov.scot/Topics/Built-Environment/planning/Appeals/howwework/
    guidanceforreporters

be mirrored at a local level would it not have been better to refer to a 'local appeal body' as opposed to a 'local review body'?

It would have been better if the Scottish Government had addressed the uncertainties about decision-making by amending the relevant legislation rather than, for example, asserting through the July 2011 letter from its Chief Planner that the '*de novo*' approach should be adopted in determining cases brought before local review bodies.

However, regulation 22 of the 2013 Regulations requires the local review body to give a decision notice which includes 'details of the provisions of the development plan and any other material considerations to which the local review body had regard in determining the application'. In determining the application sections 37(2) and 25 of the 1997 Act are relevant. Section 25 of the 1997 Act states:

> 'Where, in making any determination under the planning Acts, regard is to be had to the development plan, the determination is, unless material considerations indicate otherwise—
>   (a) to be made in accordance with that plan'.

Section 43B(2) of the 1997 Act further provides that the provision about matters which may be raised in a review under section 43A(8) of the 1997 Act does not affect any requirements or entitlement to have regard to the development plan or any other material considerations.

Therefore a local review body, when determining a 'local development' planning application which has previously been determined (including a deemed refusal) by its appointed officer, must consider the relevant provisions of the development plan and material considerations, even if they were not raised at the time of the original application and/or any subsequent decision by the appointed officer. In so doing the local review body must:

- identify the provisions of the development plan which are relevant to the determination of the application being considered;
- properly interpret those provisions – this is a matter of law (policies should be interpreted objectively in accordance with

the language used, read as always in its proper context, but should not be construed as if they were statutory or contractual provisions);

- consider whether or not the proposal accords with the development plan;
- identify and consider relevant material considerations both for and against the proposal; and
- assess whether, on balance, those considerations warrant the grant of planning permission for a proposed development although it is contrary to the development plan, or the refusal of planning permission for a proposed development albeit that it accords with the development plan.[34]

The appointed officer's 'report on handling' (if any) is just one of the 'review documents' which a local review body will have to consider.

A 'local review body', in determining a 'local development' planning application, will require to make its decision pursuant to sections 37(2) and 25 of the 1997 Act and in so doing is not restricted to either considering the evidence on which the appointed officer's decision was made[35] or considering whether that decision was 'appropriate'.

Therefore it appears that a local review body must determine the 'local development' application on the basis of the development plan and other material considerations based on the material before it, and not simply review the material that was before the appointed officer and consider whether that officer's decision (if any) was 'appropriate'.

---

34 See 1997 Act, s 25 and, eg, *City of Edinburgh Council v Secretary of State for Scotland* [1997] UKHL 38; *Tesco Stores Ltd v Dundee City Council* [2012] UKSC 13; *R (on the application of Cherkley Campaign Ltd) v Mole Valley District Council* [2014] EWCA Civ 567.
35 See also 2013 Regulations, reg 17 (New evidence) referred to in Chapter 7.

Chapter 4

Preparing and Submitting a Notice of Review and Period for its Determination

This chapter addresses the submission of a notice of review requiring the planning authority (through its local review body) to review the case under section 43A(8) of the 1997 Act and related provisions including the period for determining a review.

Should the applicant issue a notice of review or a notice of appeal?

Section 43A(8) of the 1997 Act provides that the applicant for planning permission, or for consent, agreement or approval required by a condition on such permission has a right to require the planning authority (through its local review body) to review the case.[1] The right arises where a proposed 'local development' falling within a scheme of delegation made under section 43A(1) of the 1997 Act has been:

- refused by an appointed officer;
- granted subject to conditions; or
- has not been determined within the period allowed for determination – four months where environmental impact assessment is required to be submitted as part of the application and otherwise two months after the validation date or any extended period agreed upon in writing by the applicant and the appointed officer.

1 1997 Act, s 43A(8)(c) (as amended from 2 February 2013 by Public Services Reform (Planning) (Local Review Procedure) (Scotland) Order 2013 (SSI 2013/24)); 1997 Act, s 43A(9), and the 2013 Regulations, reg 8(2).

Appointed officer refuses 'local development' planning permission application or grants it subject to conditions

Where the appointed officer determines an application for 'local development' planning permission, or a related consent, agreement or approval required by such a permission by refusing it or granting it subject to conditions the planning authority's decision notice must be accompanied by a prescribed form of notice.[2] That notice sets out the applicant's right to require the planning authority to review the case within three months beginning with the date of the decision notice. It must also be accompanied by a statement explaining how the applicant may obtain information about how to require a review of the case by the planning authority's local review body under section 43A(8) of the 1997 Act. So in any case of such a refusal or conditional grant of an application it should be clear that the applicant may require the planning authority to review the case (and cannot make an appeal under section 47 of the 1997 Act to the Scottish Ministers via the Scottish Government's Directorate for Planning and Environmental Appeals ('DPEA')).

However, it is possible that the decision notice issued by a planning authority either omits the relevant wording or, in error, directs the applicant to the wrong method of disputing the decision. In 2013–14 the DPEA had 'no remit' in 35 cases where planning permission appeals were made. Most, if not all, of those cases will be cases where the applicant should have issued a 'notice of review' to the planning authority rather than a 'notice of appeal' to the DPEA.

Failure to determine 'local development' planning application

In the case of failure to determine the 'local development' planning application it may not in fact be clear which decision-making route the planning authority was going to take in relation to the application.

---

2 Town and Country Planning (Development Management Procedure) (Scotland) Regulations 2013 (SSI 2013/155), reg 28(4)(a) and Sch 6 (Form 1).

As explained in Chapter 2, schemes of delegation for local development planning applications will often have triggers for the matter to be determined at committee. It may not be clear whether these triggers would have taken the application outwith the appointed person's delegated powers (for instance there may have been more than the requisite number of objections to the application) and this, in turn, required that the decision be taken at committee and, therefore, that the planning application would properly be the subject of an appeal to the DPEA.

If there is any doubt on the matter, clarification should be sought from the planning authority well in advance of the time limits for lodging either a notice of appeal or a notice of review.

Time limits for lodging a notice of review

The time limits within which a notice of review has to be lodged vary according to the basis on which the review is being made.

A review against a refusal of planning permission or against its conditional grant is to be made within the period of three months beginning with the date of the notice of the decision to which the review relates.

In the case of a review against non-determination of the application, the time limit is more nuanced. Normally planning authorities have two months after the validation date of any application for planning permission to determine it. However, in the case of an application for planning permission for an 'EIA development',[3] the planning authority has four months after the validation date to determine it.[4]

Any notice of review relating to non-determination must be served within three months beginning with the date of the notice of the decision to which the review relates, or the date of expiry of the period allowed for determination of the application (as the case may be); in other words, within three months of the two-month

---

3 Defined by Town and Country Planning (Environmental Impact Assessment) (Scotland) Regulations 2011 (SSI 2011/139), reg 2(1).
4 2013 Regulations, reg 8(2).

period or the four-month period (as the case may be) which the planning authority had to determine the application.[5]

From 2 February 2013 section 43A(8)(c) of the 1997 Act has allowed the prescribed two-month and four-month periods to be extended by agreement in writing between the applicant and the appointed officer.[6] However, any such written agreement must be concluded within the prescribed period and thereafter within any extended period(s).[7]

In all cases, the term 'within' suggests that any notice of review should be received by the planning authority before the end of the requisite number of calendar months.[8] So, for example, where an applicant wishes to review a decision notice dated 10 January, the notice of review and related papers should be in the hands of the planning authority on or before 9 April.

Completing a notice of review

A notice of review must be given on the form obtained from the planning authority. The notice of review form obtained from most planning authorities is based on a model form produced by the Scottish Government in 2009.[9]

The requirements for a notice of review are set out in the 2013 Regulations. Regulation 9(3) states:

'The notice of review (on a form obtained from the planning authority) must include—
    (a) the name and address of the applicant;
    (b) the date and the reference number of the application in respect of which the review is required;
    (c) the name and address of the representative of the applicant

---

5 2013 Regulations, reg 9(2).
6 Public Services Reform (Planning) (Local Review Procedure) (Scotland) Order 2013 (SSI 2013/24).
7 *Vattenfall Wind Power Ltd v Scottish Ministers* [2009] CSIH 27.
8 Interpretation Act 1978, Sch 1 makes it clear that a month is a calendar month for these purposes.
9 See e-planning Scotland at eplanning.scotland.gov.uk/WAM/paperforms.htm

(if any) and whether any notice or other correspondence which is required by these regulations to be sent to the applicant should be sent to the representative instead of the applicant; and

(d) a statement setting out the applicant's reasons for requiring the local review body to review the case and by what, if any, procedure (or combination of procedures) mentioned in regulation 13(4) the applicant considers the review should be conducted.'

Other important points to bear in mind when drafting the notice of review are set out in sub-paragraphs (4) and (5) of regulation 9 which state:

'(4) Subject to paragraph (5)—

(a) all matters which the applicant intends to raise in the review must be set out in the notice of review or in the documents which accompany the notice of review; and

(b) all documents, materials and evidence which the applicant intends to rely on in the review must accompany the notice of review.

(5) In addition to matters set out in the notice of review and documents which accompany the notice of review, the applicant may raise matters and submit further documents, materials or evidence only in accordance with and to the extent permitted by regulation 15 and the Hearing Session Rules.'

This latter provision, in particular, puts a strict obligation on the applicant for review (and any applicant's agent) to get things right first time. If an important document were missed in the submission of the review, then a planning authority would be entitled to refuse its later submission. Beyond the notice of review and any documents that accompany it, the only other opportunity an applicant may be given is if the local review body decides in terms of regulation 15 of the 2013 Regulations that further written representations are required, or a hearing is to be held in terms of the 'Hearing Session Rules' set out in Schedule 1 to the 2013 Regulations.

The planning authority's application form itself should, if it does not follow the Scottish Government style, at least give the applicant the opportunity to include all the information required by regulation 9(3) of the 2013 Regulations.

Notice of review form

The first page of the Scottish Government form of the notice of review deals with requirements (a), (b) and (c) under regulation 9(3) of the 2013 Regulations. On the second page, it sets out the different types of application which might be subject to a review, namely:

- an application for planning permission (including householder application);
- an application for planning permission in principle;
- further application (including development that has not yet commenced and where a time limit has been imposed; renewal of planning permission; and/or modification, variation or removal of a planning condition); and
- application for approval of matters specified in conditions.

Although this is not strictly necessary, it is suggested that it is useful information at this stage. Even more useful is the next section, which asks the applicant to specify whether the review is being sought on the basis of: a refusal of the application by the appointed officer; failure by the appointed officer to determine the application within the period allowed (including an agreed extended period) for determination of the application; or conditions imposed on a consent by an appointed officer.

Review procedure

The next section of the Scottish Government form covers one half of regulation 9(3)(d) of the 2013 Regulations, by asking the applicant to indicate what procedure or combination of procedures is most appropriate in the applicant's opinion for handling of the review, namely: further written submissions; hearing sessions; site inspection; or assessment of review documents only, with no further procedure.

Regulation 9(3)(d) provides that the notice of review must include a statement setting out by what procedure or combination of procedures the applicant considers the review should be conducted. A question might arise as to whether, for instance, an applicant by completing this section of the relevant form and selecting procedures other than a hearing is waiving the guaranteed right under ECHR Article 6(1) to a public hearing.[10] It might be considered that fulfilling the legislative requirement to articulate what the applicant considers to be the most appropriate procedure for the handling of the particular review is not an 'unequivocal' waiver of the right to a public hearing. The uncertainty about this may lead to an applicant seeking to retain the option of pursuing arguments about ECHR Article 6(1) compliance by indicating that one or more hearing sessions is the appropriate procedure for handling the review.

This is a key opportunity for the applicant (and the applicant's agent) to try to influence the decision by the local review body as to the procedure to be used in determining the review. Before completing the appropriate section of the notice of review form it may be useful for the applicant (and the applicant's agent) to consider the terms of the DPEA's *Reporter Guidance Note 7: No further procedure*[11] and its *Reporter Guidance Note 8: Deciding further procedure.*[12]

Ultimately, it is a decision for the local review body whether procedure beyond an assessment of review documents at only a single meeting is required.[13] It is difficult to imagine a situation where the applicant would know at this stage that further written submissions would be needed. Asking for one or more hearing sessions will at least give the applicant an opportunity to present the case before the local review body although, in practice, many local review bodies do not hold hearing sessions routinely, and the applicant should set out as fully as possible why this option has been selected.

It is perhaps more easy to articulate why a site inspection is needed, particularly where an assessment of things such as road safety issues at a junction may have come into the original decision.

10 *Chhokar v Secretary of State for Communities and Local Government* [2014] EWHC 3155 (Admin). See also, eg, *Di Placito v Slater* [2003] EWCA Civ 1863 at para 51.

11 www.gov.scot/Resource/0045/00458559.pdf

12 www.gov.scot/Resource/0045/00458560.pdf

13 See *Carroll v Scottish Borders Council* [2014] CSOH 6 at para 38.

Again, a full explanation should be given at this stage for the reasoning behind the applicant's request.

The standard Scottish Government form then goes on to ask further questions on the feasibility of a site inspection, whether the site can be viewed entirely from public land and if it is possible for the site to be accessed safely.

The form then asks if there are reasons why the applicant thinks the local review body would be unable to undertake an accompanied site inspection and, if so, to explain them. Routinely, site inspections would be unaccompanied and it will normally be the review body's preference as it is easier to demonstrate that the local review body has not been unduly influenced by the applicant, or indeed any other party, if they are not present at the site inspection.

Statement of the applicant's case

The next part of the Scottish Government form deals with the last of the requirements under regulation 9(3)(d) of the 2013 Regulations by leaving space for a statement setting out the applicant's reasons for requiring the local review body to review the case. Although the form leaves a space of about half a page for the applicant or agent to do so, it is likely, in most cases, that the applicant's statement of case will be provided in a separate document.

New matters

The form then asks if the applicant has raised any matters which were not before the appointed officer at the time the officer's determination was made. If so, the applicant is asked to explain why the new material is being raised, why it was not raised with the appointed officer before the application was determined, and why it should now be considered in the review. It appears that the reference in the notice of review form to 'material' is incorrect as it does not properly reflect section 43B of the 1997 Act which does not refer to 'material'. Further any new matter, and related material, will generally have to be considered as falling within section 43B(2) of the 1997 Act which provides that section 43B(1) of the 1997 Act does not affect 'any requirement or entitlement to have regard to (a) the provisions of the development plan, or (b) any other material considerations'.

The issue of matters that may be raised in a review under section 43A(8) of the 1997 Act has been addressed in more detail in Chapter 3.

An applicant should consider whether there is any new matter which the local review body ought to consider and explain why it should be considered by the local review body. This is particularly important, given that if the local review body is to determine the application at the first meeting, there is really no other opportunity in terms of the legislative scheme for such an explanation to be put forward, although the applicant could, in discussions with the planning authority's staff, ask for reasons to be put forward.

If the planning authority's officers consider that new matter is raised then the planning authority should ask for an explanation from the applicant if no explanation has been provided.

The circumstances will vary from case to case. It may be, for example, in a non-determination case, that matters were raised by consultees or objectors which the applicant could only subsequently address as part of a notice of review. Alternatively, there could be a material change of circumstances such as the grant of planning permission in another similar case which may give rise to a submission about inconsistency in decision-making or changes in the locality since the application was submitted or determined and such changes might provide a different context for issues such as amenity or overlooking and privacy. In any such event, the applicant will have to make a submission to the local review body about why the matter is being raised now, as opposed to its being raised with the appointed officer, and that submission may be based on the statutory exception about any failure to raise the matter being a consequence of exceptional circumstances.

List of documents and evidence

The last page of the form gives space for a list of any supporting documents, materials and evidence, supplies a useful checklist to ensure the applicant has provided everything, and requires the applicant or the applicant's agent to sign the application to confirm the giving of notice to the planning authority to review the 'local development' application specified therein.

If new documents, material or evidence have been submitted with the notice of review, then the planning authority's officers may wish to seek an explanation if no explanation is provided in the notice of review.

Disclosure of information relating to national security

Regulation 18 of the 2013 Regulations makes provision that withholding information from a notice of review about national security or measures taken, or to be taken, to ensure the security of any premises or property does not invalidate the notice of review. A written statement, including a statement that disclosure of the information would be contrary to the national interest, has to accompany the notice of review.

If the local review body is unable to determine the review without the withheld information, then the case could be called in for determination by Scottish Ministers, and special procedures for dealing with national security sensitive information applied.[14]

Further copies of documents etc

Regulation 19 of the 2013 Regulations allows a local review body to require any person who has submitted 'documents, materials or evidence' in connection with the review to provide such number of additional copies as the local review body specifies and provide them to such other persons as the local review body specifies. This is potentially an onerous requirement on the applicant, and should not be used by local review body staff to routinely put the burden of photocopying relatively short applications for review onto the applicant.

---

14 Circular 5/2013: *Schemes of Delegation and Local Reviews*, para 27.

However, if applicants are to submit large complex documents for submission with the review and the planning authority still operates a paper-based system for agendas, it may be reasonable for the planning authority staff to request additional copies.

One practical difficulty which the legislation does not provide for in the case of local reviews is access to the relevant development plan policies. This has, in practice, led to some applicants for review submitting either copies of the relevant policies or, in some cases, the whole plan, to ensure that the local review body has all the necessary documentation in front of it.

In practice, this should not normally be necessary, and it would be iniquitous if applicants for review were asked, under regulation 19, to submit copies of the planning authority's own documentation.

It is worth noting that the 'review documents' have to be made available by the planning authority until a review is determined and that they have to be considered by the local review body.[15] The definition of 'review documents' in the 2013 Regulations includes not just the 'report on handling' but 'any documents referred to in that report', so an applicant for review should have reasonable confidence that the relevant development plan provisions will be made available to the local review body (unless the appointed officer has completely missed relevant references to the development plan in the report). It would be helpful if planning authorities that have bespoke forms of notices of review specify in those forms that the relevant development plan policies will be available for the local review body and, in turn, minimise waste in terms of copying planning authority documents.

Time limits for determination of the review

Whether an application for review relates to the refusal of a planning application, or its grant subject to conditions which are deemed unacceptable, there is no prescribed time limit within which the local review body requires to determine it. There is a

15 2013 Regulations, regs 11 and 12.

requirement to issue its decision within a reasonable time.[16] The time limits within which certain steps of all reviews of this nature have to be carried out are addressed in the next chapter.

However, in the case of a requirement for review as a result of non-determination of the 'local development' application by an appointed officer, section 43A(17) of the 1997 Act and regulation 8(3) of the 2013 Regulations provide that the time limit is the period of three months beginning on the date when the requirement to review is made by virtue of section 43A(8)(c) of the 1997 Act. The provisions of section 43A(17) are worth considering in full:

'(17) Where a requirement to review is made by virtue of paragraph (c) of subsection (8) and the planning authority have not conducted the review within such period as may be prescribed by regulations or a development order, the authority are to be deemed to have decided to refuse the application and section 47(1) is to apply accordingly.'

It is not clear what exactly is meant by the word 'conducted'. It is not a defined term. One interpretation might be that the local review body has concluded the review and issued its decision notice. However, if that were the intent of the legislation, it is not clear why the subsection would not simply refer to issue of the decision notice.

Obligation to determine the application

Some planning authorities have taken the view that should they fail to conclude the review within the three-month period, then no further procedure should be implemented as the applicant's remedy lies elsewhere. Other planning authorities take the view that the local review body should conclude matters even if the three-month period has expired. In our view the latter approach is to be pre-

16 European Convention for the Protection of Human Rights and Fundamental Freedoms, Art 6(1) and *Lafarge Redland Aggregates Ltd v Scottish Ministers* 2001 SC 298.

ferred because of the relevant case law about a planning authority's continuing obligation to take a decision on a planning permission application – it has been said that 'the planning authority remains seised of the [planning permission] application and is obliged to make a decision on it.'[17]

So, unless the application has been taken out the hands of the local review body by way of an appeal to the Scottish Ministers or otherwise, the local review body needs to determine the case for review before it.

17 See, eg, *London and Clydeside Estates Ltd v Aberdeen District Council* 1980 SLT 81; *Bovis Homes (Scotland) Ltd v Inverclyde District Council* 1992 SLT 473; *Vattenfall Wind Power Ltd v Scottish Ministers* at para 10.

Chapter 5

Local Review Body Pre-meeting Process

This chapter considers the period from receipt of a notice of review until the case set out in that notice is first considered at a meeting of the local review body.

The 1997 Act adopts a relatively light touch about how a local planning review should be conducted. It simply stipulates that the form and procedures of any review conducted by a local review body must be set out in regulations or a development order.[1] Section 43A(11) provides that the regulations or development order may:

- make different provision for different cases or classes of case and for different stages of a case;
- make provision in relation to oral or written submissions and to documents in support of such submissions and for time limits (including a time limit for requiring the review); and
- require the planning authority to give to the person who has required the review such notice as may be prescribed by the regulations or the order as to the manner in which that review has been dealt with.

Section 43A(13) also allows the regulations or order to make provision as to:

- the making of oral submissions, or as to any failure to make such submissions or to lodge documents in support of such submissions; or

1 1997 Act, s 43A(10).

- the lodging of, or as to any failure to lodge, written submissions or documents in support of such submissions,

and, subject to section 43B, as to what matters may be raised in the course of the review.

Finally, section 43A(14) allows the regulations or order to provide that the manner in which the review, or any stage of the review, is to be conducted (as for example whether oral submissions are to be made or written submissions lodged) is to be at the discretion of the planning authority.

The steps a planning authority has to take following receipt of a notice of review are set out in the Town and Country Planning (Schemes of Delegation and Local Review Procedure) (Scotland) Regulations 2013 ('the 2013 Regulations').[2]

Pre-meeting procedures: resources

The first steps a local review body requires to take following receipt of a notice of review are purely administrative. While the wording throughout the 2013 Regulations is that the local review body itself carries out the various administrative steps involved, there is no suggestion that these could not properly be carried out by planning authority officers on behalf of the local review body as opposed to members of that body.

Practices vary as to which members of the planning authority's staff take overall charge of the administration of the local review body's work, although, in general, it is staff within the authority's administrative or democratic, as opposed to planning, services. This is entirely appropriate given the need to maintain separation between the staff in planning services involved in the appointed officer's decision, and the administration and operation of the local review body. However, there will be some steps which will require some planning expertise and the planning authority should consider carefully who does what to avoid any unnecessary delays or potential confusion.

2 SSI 2013/157.

Does the local review body have jurisdiction?

Consideration needs to be given to whether the local review body has jurisdiction to consider the 'local development' application that is the subject of the notice of review.

In the case of non-determination of the 'local development' application by the appointed officer are there, for instance, so many objections that the application could not have been determined under delegated powers by the appointed officer?

Has the notice of review been served on the local review body within the period of three months beginning with:

- the date of the notice of decision to which the review relates;
- the date of expiry of the period allowed for determination of the application by the appointed officer (in the case of an application for planning permission for EIA development, the period of four months after the validation date and in any other cases two months after the validation date)[3] or the period agreed for the determination of the application?[4]

Compliance with the development management procedures

Have the specific development management procedures been complied with?

Where, for whatever reason, the relevant development management procedures were not complied with prior to receipt of the notice of review, the local review body must complete these. Regulation 20 of the 2013 Regulations provides:

'The local review body must, to the extent not already done so, comply with regulations 18 (notification by the planning authority), 19 (notification of minerals applications), 20 (publication of application by the planning authority) and 25 (consultation by the planning authority) of the Town and Country Planning (Develop-

3 2013 Regulations, regs 8 and 9(2).
4 1997 Act, s 43A(8)(c) as amended by Public Services Reform (Planning) (Local Review Procedure) (Scotland) Order 2013 (SSI 2013/24). See also *Vattenfall Wind Power Ltd v Scottish Ministers* [2009] CSIH 27.

ment Management Procedure) (Scotland) Regulations 2013[5] before determining the review.'

Although it is not specifically stated in the Regulations, it would seem obvious that the terms of regulation 20 have to be carried out in advance of any meeting of the local review body to look at the application. For example, if the neighbour notification of a 'local development' permission planning application has never been carried out, then all of the provisions relating to an 'interested party' would become meaningless.

Acknowledgement of notice of review and notifying interested parties

Regulation 10(1) of the 2013 Regulations sets out the requirements that the local review body must, not later than 14 days following notification of the review:

- send an acknowledgement of the notice of review to the applicant and inform the applicant how documents related to the review may be inspected; and
- give notice of the review to each 'interested party', namely:
  - any authority or person consulted by the planning authority in compliance with a requirement imposed by virtue of section 43(1)(c) of the 1997 Act and from whom the planning authority received representations (which were not subsequently withdrawn) in connection with the application; and
  - any other person from whom the planning authority received representations (which were not subsequently withdrawn) in connection with the application, before the end of the period mentioned in section 38(1) of the 1997 Act.[6]

If there is no 'interested party' the only requirements are to issue an acknowledgement to the applicant of receipt of the notice of review and to provide information about the inspection of documents.

5 SSI 2013/155.
6 2013 Regulations, reg 2.

If there is an 'interested party' then any such person will fall into one of two categories: those who require to be notified in terms of section 43(1)(c) of the 1997 Act, being a prescribed person, body or authority, such as Scottish Water, who must be consulted in specified circumstances;[7] and any other person who made representations within the prescribed period and did not subsequently withdraw them. The prescribed periods are:

- within 28 days where the 'local development' application has been processed under the Town and Country Planning (Environmental Impact Assessment) (Scotland) Regulations 2011 ('the 2011 Regulations') beginning with the date of a notice under regulation 17 of the 2011 Regulations;[8] and
- in all other cases not less than 21 days for proposed developments that are not EIA development.[9]

The slightly complex wording of the notification provisions and the accompanying definition of an 'interested party' perhaps masks a fairly easily defined group of persons. It is those persons who made representations on the original planning application timeously, whether they were consulted or not. This makes regulation 10(2) of the 2013 Regulations slightly more elaborate than perhaps it needs to be:

'Notice under paragraph (1)(b) may be given to each interested party—
  (a) by post to any interested party notified or consulted under the [1997] Act other than by newspaper advertisement; and
  (b) by post or by advertisement in a newspaper circulating the locality where the proposed development is situated, to any other interested party.'

---

7 Town and Country Planning (Development Management Procedure) (Scotland) Regulations 2013 (SSI 2013/155) ('the 2013 DMR'), reg 25 and Sch 5.
8 SSI 2011/139.
9 1997 Act, ss 34(4)(a) and 38(1) as applied by the 2013 DMR, reg 18(3)(g).

It should be clear who are the persons who have made representations to the 'local development' planning application, and normally a planning authority would insist on such persons having given a name and address for the representation to be treated as valid. If that is the case, it would seem slightly strange if the local review body gave notice by way of advertisement, and normal good practice would seem to be to notify any interested party by post.

Sub-paragraph (3) of regulation 10 of the 2013 Regulations then sets out the minimum requirements for the notice to be given to each interested party. The notice should:

- state the name of the applicant and the address of the site to which the review relates;
- describe the application;
- state that copies of any representations previously made in respect of the application will be considered by the local review body when determining the review;
- state that further representations may be made to the local review body and include information as to how any representations may be made, by what date they must be made and that a copy of the representations will be sent to the applicant for comment; and
- state how a copy of the notice of review and other documents relating to the review may be inspected.

Response to notice of review by an 'interested party'

Once notice has been given to an interested party, there is a 14-day period within which they may make representations in respect of the review to the review body.[10] This is a mandatory 14-day period, and there does not appear to be any ability for the planning authority to extend it. The phrase 'the date on which notice is given' suggests that the usual two-day period for post should be allowed when calculating the 14 days.

It may be that an 'interested party' is content to simply rest on

10 2013 Regulations, reg 10(4).

the representations made about the application. Those representations will be part of the papers considered by the local review body.

If an 'interested party' makes further representations subparagraphs (5) and (6) of regulation 10 of the 2013 Regulations are relevant. They provide that the local review body must send a copy of any representations received in response to the earlier notice to the applicant, and must inform the applicant how and by what date (which date should be not less than 14 days after the date on which such copy is sent) the applicant may make comments to the local review body on the representations, whereupon the applicant may make comments. Here, the 14-day period is slightly different in that it runs from the date the notice is sent and there is no upper limit to how long the applicant has to respond – it is to be not less than 14 days but could be a longer period. An illustrated example might best work through these provisions. In the case of a notice of review received on 1 March:

- the local review body administrators must send an acknowledgement to the applicant by 15 March;
- also by 15 March, the local review body administrator should send a notice to any interested party requiring a response by, if the notice is sent on 15 March, 1 April;
- should representations be received by 1 April, then a notice should be sent to the applicant requiring any comments on those representations and that notice should allow until at least 15 April for comments; and
- if the deadline for an applicant's comments is 15 April, by 16 April, the authority will be in a position to assemble all the papers for the first meeting of the local review body to consider the review.

Publication of review documents

Regulation 11 of the 2013 Regulations states:

'(1) The planning authority must, in relation to a review, make a copy of—
    (a) the review documents;

(b) any notice given under regulation 10(1); and

(c) any procedure notice,

available for inspection at an office of the planning authority until such time as the review is determined.

(2) The planning authority are until such time as a review is determined to afford to any person who so requests the opportunity to inspect and, where practicable, take copies of any review documents (or any part thereof).'

Having the review documents and associated notices available for inspection at an office of the planning authority should, in the modern digital age, be the bare minimum requirement for a planning authority. Most authorities now have well-developed online planning presences and, in most cases, it should be a relatively simple task to link the relevant review documentation to the original planning application documents which have previously been made available online.

It is worth noting at this point the definition of 'review documents' which are the documents caught by this and other parts of the 2013 Regulations. Review documents are defined as being:

'notice of the decision in respect of which the application to which the review relates, the Report on Handling and any documents referred to in that Report, the notice of review given in accordance with regulation 9, all documents accompanying the notice of review in accordance with regulation 9(4) and any representations or comments made under regulation 10(4) or (6) in relation to the review.'

Note that the definition includes any documents referred to in a report on handling. This will include development plan references, although, again, these should be readily available online in most cases.

Assembly of papers for first meeting of the local review body

In the vast majority of review cases, the acknowledgement of the papers; service on those who had made representations to the original application; notification of any further representations to the applicant; and ingathering of the applicant's further comments will be the full extent of the procedure following receipt of a notice of review. Thereafter the local review body is in a position to decide how the case under review is to proceed. Decisions of this nature must be taken by the review body in public.[11] The usual requirements for notice of meetings discussed in Chapter 3 will apply but, in addition, regulation 7(4) of the 2013 Regulations makes it clear that the applicant and interested parties are to be given 'such notice of the date, time and place fixed for the holding of such meeting (and any subsequent variation thereof) as may appear to the local review body to be reasonable in the circumstances'.

As explained in Chapter 3, the local review body is a committee of the planning authority and, as such, any meeting should follow the requirement for an agenda setting out the cases to be considered as well as the minutes of the last meeting of the local review body. These will require to be published at least three clear days in advance of the meeting.

Beyond this point, the 2013 Regulations themselves are silent as to what papers should be put before the local review body for the first meeting. However, it would seem self-evident that they should, at the very least, consist of the review documents which, as above stated, comprise:

- the decision notice (if any);
- the report on handling (if any) and any documents referred to in it;
- the notice of review;
- all documents accompanying the notice of review; and
- any representations or comments made by interested parties and/or the applicant in terms of regulation 10 of the 2013 Regulations.

Normally the review documents should give sufficient information for the local review body to at least decide whether there are any unresolved questions which require further procedure. It would be

---

11 2013 Regulations, reg 7(2).

competent for a local review body's planning adviser, for example, to include additional material such as a report commenting on the review documents. However, that hardly seems necessary. The report on handling and associated documents will set out the appointed officer's reasoning for the original decision as will, on a more formal basis, the decision notice. The notice of review and its accompanying documents should ideally set out the applicant's full case.

Timetabling meetings and pre-meetings

Now that the legislation has had some years of practice, it is likely that planning authorities will have a reasonable idea of how much time and effort is required to resource the local review body and, specifically, how often it needs to meet to despatch its business efficiently. A timetable of meetings of the local review body will normally be available and, again, experience should have shown how many review cases can be dealt with comfortably at a single meeting. Administrators will want to have regard to the particular characteristics of each case and schedule them in accordingly.

Pre-meeting briefings

At this point, it is worth setting out the provisions of regulation 7(2) of the 2013 Regulations:

'Meetings of the local review body at which decisions—
    (a) under regulation 13 relating to the manner in which the review is to be conducted; or
    (b) as to how the case under review is to be determined, are to be held in public.'

This does not strictly deny the local review body the chance of meeting in private for a pre-meeting briefing if, at such a meeting, no decisions are made as to how the review is to be conducted or as to how it should be determined. However, pre-meetings carry a risk that the applicant or those who have made representations suspect that decisions relating to these matters are, in fact, being taken in advance behind closed doors. The next chapter will deal with the role of a planning adviser and the particular position such an adviser occupies in comparison to applicants who are unable to address the local review body. Any advice or briefing by either the planning adviser, legal adviser or the clerk of the local review body would be better given in a public forum to avoid any suspicion of such matters being discussed – and agreed in advance – in private.

Chapter 6

The First Local Review Body Meeting

It has been recognised that local review bodies need assistance to enable them to properly discharge their functions. Assistance includes receiving appropriate training, being able to call upon legal and administrative help, and to appoint a person ('an assessor') with particular specialist or technical skills so that the local review body can take an informed and lawful decision.

At the first meeting the local review body can:

- conclude that the review documents provide sufficient information and proceed to determine the application which is the subject of the notice of review;[1] or
- if it does not conclude that the review documents provide sufficient information to enable it to determine the application which is the subject of the notice of review, it can decide that the application is to be determined by means of written submissions; one or more hearing sessions; site inspection or a combination of those three procedures.[2]

Scottish Government Circular 5/2013: *Schemes of Delegation and Local Reviews* ('Circular 5/2013') expresses the expectation that the majority of cases coming before the local review body will be accompanied by sufficient information for the review to be determined quickly. However, it recognises that there will be some cases, particularly those involving non-determination of a 'local de-

---

1 2013 Regulations, reg 12.
2 2013 Regulations, reg 13.

velopment' application, where the local review body will wish to obtain further information by means of one or more of written submissions, a hearing session or a site inspection.

As we noted in Chapter 3, the 2008 Scottish Government consultation paper *Modernising Planning Appeals* states that in cases of non-determination it will be necessary for advice on the planning merits of the case to be provided to the local review body and for such material to be made available to the applicant for comment.

This chapter considers both the forms of assistance available to the local review body and the decision taken at its first meeting to consider the application that is subject to the notice of review.

The first local review body meeting

Once the process following receipt of the notice of review described in Chapter 5 has been carried out, the planning authority must convene the first meeting of the local review body to consider the application that is the subject of the notice of review.

Circular 5/2013 states that membership of the local review body (including the size of a local review body) and administrative arrangements for supporting the review process are matters for the planning authority to decide.[3]

Practices will vary between planning authorities but, in general, there will be scheduled dates in the planning authority's calendar of meetings so that local review cases, when ready, can be put to the next suitable available meeting date.

The composition of the local review body will vary. Most planning authorities operate from a larger pool of potential members than will actually be required for the meeting, and typically select five members from the pool of potential members for any particular local review body meeting. The Town and Country Planning (Schemes of Delegation and Local Review Procedure) (Scotland) Regulations 2013 ('the 2013 Regulations') require that a review case is to be conducted by at least three members of the planning

---

3 Scottish Government Circular 5/2013: *Schemes of Delegation and Local Reviews* ('Circular 5/2013') paras 28 and 30.

authority.[4] Circular 5/2013 states that in cases where the local review body comprises a small number of elected members, the authority should ensure a larger pool of elected members is available to provide cover where appropriate.

The need for appropriate training to equip planning authority members to undertake their function of determining an application that is the subject of a notice of review is widely recognised. Circular 5/2013, for instance, reiterates:

'Scottish Ministers expect that arrangements put in place by planning authorities to review decisions will follow a process that is demonstrably fair and transparent. Planning authorities should ensure members participating in review cases receive appropriate training in planning issues and in holding hearing sessions. In most instances, it is likely that one local review body per planning authority will carry out the review function effectively. However, some authorities may consider that more than one local review body would provide an appropriate service, perhaps given the size of the geographic area required to be covered.'[5]

As shall be seen the Scottish Government also recognises that, notwithstanding members of local review bodies being trained in planning issues and in holding hearing sessions, the local review body may require input from relevant professionals in arriving at its decision.

However the members of the local review body are selected to consider the case that is subject of the notice of review, the requirements discussed in Chapter 3 for issue of agenda and papers, as well as the minimum requirements for papers discussed in Chapter 5, have to be followed before the first meeting of the local review body.

Administrative and professional support for the local review body

As noted above, Circular 5/2013 states that planning authorities

---

4 2013 Regulations, reg 7(1).
5 Circular 5/2013, para 30 and Circular 7/2009: *Schemes of Delegation and Local Reviews*, para 28.

should ensure that members participating in review cases receive appropriate training in planning issues and in holding hearing sessions. It also states:

> 'Planning authorities will want to ensure that the local review body are supported by appropriate administrative and legal advice to ensure that members are guided on the review process. Where the local review body consider it necessary to take further advice before reaching a decision on the review it will be for the planning authority to arrange such advice. Scottish Ministers expect that all administrative arrangements required to support the review process should respect the principles of fairness and transparency that must underpin the operation of the system.'[6]

This appears to envisage a role for specialist support (provided by an assessor) as well as administrative and legal support. It does not appear to envisage a local review body requiring support in planning issues (as appropriate training is to be given to members on planning issues). However, the 2008 Scottish Government consultation paper *Modernising Planning Appeals* suggested a need for advice on planning merits in non-determination cases. Further, the best practice guidance notes prepared by the Local Review Body Forum recognise a role for a planning adviser to the local review body.[7]

Appointment of assessors

The only statutory requirements relating to appointing advisers to the local review body are set out in regulation 21 of the 2013 Regulations. That regulation makes provision for the appointment of an assessor to sit with the local review body at a hearing session to advise on matters specified by the local review body. When the first iteration of this regulation appeared in 2008, there was much discussion as to what might be meant by 'assessor'. However, sub-

---

6 Circular 5/2013, para 31.
7 The notes are accessible at www.gov.scot/Topics/Built-Environment/ planning/aboutappeals/Bestpractice.

sequently Circular 7/2009: *Schemes of Delegation and Local Reviews* and now Circular 5/2013 state:

> 'Assessors are used infrequently in the current appeal system to advise on specialist or technical matters that are at issue. It is for the local review body to consider to what extent there is a role for a specialist assessor to sit with it at a particular hearing session.'[8]

One example of a technical issue which led to an assessor being appointed to provide assistance to one of the Scottish Ministers is the issue of olfactometry (odour).[9] However, there may be a greater need for the appointment of an assessor by a local review body (particularly in non-determination cases) for more routine matters such as retail impact assessments and the sequential approach.

It seems clear, therefore, that an assessor is meant to be a person skilled on particular technical matters and who is not either a planning adviser or a legal adviser. Further, the appointment of an assessor is restricted to cases that are being considered by the holding of one or more hearing sessions.

The role of planning advisers and legal advisers

The 2013 Regulations do not say anything about the appointment of planning advisers or legal advisers. As noted above, Circular 5/2013, at paragraph 31, states that planning authorities will want to ensure that the local review body is supported by 'appropriate administrative and legal advice'. However, the need for the local review body to have planning advice is highlighted by a best practice guidance note about the role of planning and legal advisers prepared by the Local Review Body Forum.[10]

The best practice guidance note points out that the principal role of both planning advisers and legal advisers is to guide the members of the local review body through the review documents, to respond to factual issues that arise and to advise on the relevant law but not to take part in the decision-making process.

8 At para 53.
9 See DPEA Reference PPA-130-62 (land south of High Bogany, Rothesay).
10 www.gov.scot/Resource/0038/00389407.pdf

The planning adviser

The Local Review Body Forum best practice guidance recommends that the planning adviser:

- should never be the appointed officer or the case officer – if a planning authority employee, it is best practice that the adviser has no direct input into the assessment or determination of 'local development' planning applications;
- a planning adviser should provide informative, factual information to the local review body – the adviser must ensure that they are always seen to operate in a professional manner and should guard against expressing any personal views or 'leading' the local review body in the decision-making process and any advice should never take the form of a recommendation or statement about whether or not a development complies with planning policy;
- should not introduce any written reports, assessments or oral evidence during a meeting in a way that could be construed as new evidence or matters that should previously have been circulated to interested parties – care should be taken about the use of photographs and it is good practice to ensure that the applicant has seen, and had an opportunity to comment on, all information, including photographs that will be presented to the local review body;
- will, consistent with the adviser's professional duty, bring to the attention of the local review body any 'material consideration' that has hitherto not been identified for the local review body – it is for the local review body to decide how to proceed – in the interests of natural justice, it will, in most instances, be appropriate to seek the views of parties on this additional material before proceeding to a determination; and
- should ideally be a member of the Royal Town Planning Institute with experience in development management.

The advice takes cognisance of the fact that, at the first meeting, the planning adviser's role will be subject to public scrutiny and that all advice should be given openly, fairly and without any indication of preference for the decision the local review body should take. If the local review body appears to be minded to reverse or vary the decision taken by the appointed officer, the planning adviser should be very careful about giving advice that might be perceived as trying to dissuade the local review body from that course of action. This is especially the case given that the planning adviser, like the legal adviser, will be allowed to speak at this first meeting, when neither the applicant nor interested parties (or their representatives) will be allowed to speak.

The legal adviser

The Local Review Body Forum best practice guidance note has more to say about the role of the legal adviser. The legal adviser

- must act at all times in a professional manner and must provide advice on the law including the statutory powers and duties of the local review body;
- may give a view or an opinion on points of law but should not express a view or recommend an outcome in respect of the review application – the legal adviser may, for example, advise whether or not a matter is a 'new matter' and what tests the local review body should apply before accepting it in evidence, but not whether it should be accepted in evidence;
- should not have previously given advice on the case which is under review; and
- should ideally be an enrolled solicitor in Scotland with planning law and court or tribunal experience.

It cannot be stressed enough that the legal adviser should be not just independent but be seen to be as independent as possible. In smaller planning authorities, it may be difficult for more than one solicitor in the planning authority to obtain and retain any sort of specialism in planning law. However, it would be unfortunate if the same legal adviser who had discussed matters with the appointed officer in advance of determination of the original planning application were to then be advising the local review body. If at all possible, the planning authority ought to consider appointing another solicitor with experience of planning matters.

Role of the Chair and members of the local review body

The role of Chair of a local review body is a far more onerous one than the Chair of most local authority committees. In a conventional committee setting, the Chair can rely upon officers to provide by means of a written report to the committee, and subsequent verbal input, a recommendation on the best course of action for the committee in the particular circumstances under consideration. Standing what has been said about the role of the planning advisers and legal advisers at meetings of a local review body, however, support normally available to other committees is not available to the Chair of a local review body who must, in the interests of fairness, be seen to be leading the discussion and debate on the application for review in a way that will be unfamiliar even to the most experienced of committee Chairs.

The Local Review Body Forum has produced a best practice guidance note about the role of the Chair and members of the local review bodies.[11]

The Chair of the local review body also has to ensure that the local review body reaches a decision that is transparent to the extent that what has been said at the initial meeting (or subsequent ones) reflects the reasoning of the local review body so that it can be written down in the eventual decision notice. In other words, the committee Chair has to ensure that the local review body thinks out loud and gives reasons there and then for its views.

All of the above is in addition to the Chair's usual responsibilities to ensure good order in the meeting, to draw together various strands of debate to get the sense of the meeting's decision, and to ensure that the meeting generally progresses in accordance with correct procedure. That being the case, there is much to be said for the Chair at the very least, if not all persons present at the local review body meeting, being provided with guidance notes on procedure. At the initial stage, the following points should be addressed:

---

11 www.gov.scot/Resource/0038/00389405.pdf

- it should be clear at the start of the meeting who is to chair it, particularly if the local review body has a pool of Chairs available and more than one is present;
- the Chair should introduce the elected members and advisers for the benefit of the public and clarify roles; and
- the Chair should outline the procedure set down for the meeting and ask members if they have any points requiring clarification.

It would then normally be the case that the minutes of the previous meeting would be taken and any declarations of interest be ascertained.

Initial procedural decisions

Whether the Chair of the local review body or an officer provides the initial outline of the first review case to be considered at the meeting, it is advisable that, at this stage, some initial procedural decisions are taken. In particular, regard should be had to regulation 12 of the 2013 Regulations. This states that where the local review body considers the review documents contain sufficient information to enable it to determine matters, it can do so without further procedure. In deciding whether the application that is the subject of the notice of review can be decided without further procedure, the local review body may wish to have regard to guidance issued by the Scottish Government's Directorate for Planning and Environmental Appeals ('DPEA') *Reporter Guidance Note 7 – No further procedure.*[12] That note provides examples of circumstances where it may be considered that no further procedure is necessary. The stated circumstances include, for instance, where:

- there is no dispute about the relevance of a planning policy, but the key issue relates to whether material considerations tip the balance in favour of a decision that is contrary to the development plan; and
- the physical characteristics of the site have no bearing on the issues being considered.

12 www.gov.scot/Resource/0045/00458559.pdf

It is important to make the decision about whether or not further procedure is required early if the local review body is able to do so at that stage. If, for example, written submissions on further information are required or perhaps a site inspection, then the decision to obtain information by these other means can be taken by the local review body at this stage and no further consideration of the case need happen at this point. The advantage of an early decision about whether any further procedure is required without delving too deeply into the details of the case is that the same local review body members would not need to be present the next time the case is considered with the benefit of the site visit or written submissions.

However, if the local review body, at this stage, is to explore the merits of the case in any detail, then adjourning it to a meeting with a different membership would be very difficult given that some of the information which has been drawn out at the initial meeting would not be available to all the members at the subsequent meeting. Accordingly, any decision eventually made might be perceived to be flawed.

The most common additional way of gathering information which the members might request would be a site inspection. There is some divergence of views as to whether a site inspection could be arranged in advance of the initial meeting. Clearly, this avoids unnecessary postponements of the case. However, regulation 7(2) of the 2013 Regulations states that meetings of the local review body at which decisions under regulation 13 relating to the manner in which the review is to be conducted or as to how the case under review is to be determined, are to be held in public. One interpretation of regulation 7(2) is that it would deny the local review body administrator the chance to arrange a site inspection in advance, perhaps in consultation with the Chair. However, another view is that the risk of challenge to such an advance site inspection is relatively small given that few applicants would object to the local review body having as much information before it as possible.

Another key decision to be reached is whether any new matter has been raised and, if so, whether it is admissible. The Chair will wish to take advice from the planning and legal advisers on this point (including the provisions of section 43B of the 1997 Act), although the decision must be seen to be that of the local review body.

If the local review body is content that it can proceed without further information and after it has decided whether any new matter has been raised, and whether it is admissible or not, then the Chair of the local review body can indicate that the substance of the review case itself can be considered.

Procedure after decision that there is sufficient information to determine the review

Assuming the local review body considers it has enough information to allow it to proceed to determine the case there and then, there are a range of options as to how the meeting should then progress. One is for the planning adviser to present a report, verbal or otherwise, which outlines the applicant's case as well as the reasoning behind the appointed officer's decision. Alternatively, the planning adviser might simply give a powerpoint presentation of photographs and plans of the site to give members the context.

The Chair and the other local review body members ought to have read the papers in advance, and they may have questions for either the planning adviser or legal adviser. It is now that they should ask those questions and then proceed to assess the case based on the relevant materials (such as the appointed officer's report on handling and related materials, the applicant's notice of review and any representations and comments made by interested parties) and to establish the issues relevant to the local review body's determination of the review.

Copies of the relevant development plan documents should be available to the local review body members and can be referred to at this stage if there are particular points of concern regarding the interpretation of policy,[13] and whether, in fact, the proposed development complies with policy. This is the first area of potential difference from the appointed officer's decision. In the opinion of

13 *Tesco Stores Ltd v Dundee City Council* [2012] UKSC 13.

the local review body, has the appointed officer got it right in applying the policy? Inevitably there may be different interpretations of policy wording which is not as tightly drawn as legislation.

Local review body members will have to have regard not just to the existing development plan but also to other 'material considerations' including the emerging development plan, other formal or semi-formal guidance and the views of others who have made representations.

Having decided on the interpretation of planning policy, members should then bear in mind that planning decisions should be taken in accordance with the development plan unless material considerations indicate otherwise. It is the weighing of any such material considerations that usually leads to the second possible point of departure from the appointed officer's decision. Do amenity considerations outweigh the potential advantages of the development? Does a traffic impact analysis raise sufficient concerns about road safety to override the presumption in favour of development that accords with the development plan? Different members will have different views on this and, again, the role of the Chair is key in drawing debate and discussion together.

Decision on the merits

A skilful Chair will establish which way members are minded to decide in a manner which makes clear whether a vote is required on the matter or otherwise. Assuming the local review body has an odd number of members, it may well be that the minority recognise that there is little point in pursuing the vote at this stage. The local review body is not a political arena, where votes are used to indicate points of principle even if the outcome is obvious to everyone in the meeting. On the other hand, members may feel so strongly on a particular issue that they would wish to have a decision, with motions and amendments, that is minuted. In general, however, it is far better if local review body decisions are reached by consensus.

Again, given the heightened sensitivity to a local review body decision being fair, just and transparent, local review body members should remain present throughout the hearing of a single case (requesting comfort breaks if necessary between cases) to ensure that there can be no suggestion that they had not been privy to all the information brought out in the consideration of the case.

The possible challenges to a decision by the local review body are discussed in more detail in the final chapter. For now, it is only necessary to state the basics of any decision made by the local review body in terms of the surrounding common law:

- the members of the local review body should not have fettered their discretion by regarding themselves as bound in some way in advance of the decision;[14]
- the decision must not be irrational or *Wednesbury* unreasonable;[15]
- the local review body members must not demonstrate any bias or pre-determination – 'the question is whether the fair minded and informed observer, having considered the facts, would conclude that there was a real possibility that the tribunal was biased.'[16]

Once the decision has been reached, the Chair should, if possible, sum up the details of the decision, including any changes to reasons for refusal or the conditions imposed by the local review body, in such a way that the planning and legal advisers will be able to note the decision fully and incorporate all aspects of it in the subsequent decision notice.

It may be that the decision notice itself will be delegated to officers, in consultation with the Chair. However, the reasoning behind the decision and the specifics of any particular matters which the local review body would like to see addressed should be clarified there and then in public.

---

14 See, eg, *R v Waltham Forest London Borough Council ex parte Baxter* [1988] 2 WLR 257.

15 *Associated Provincial Picture Houses Ltd v Wednesbury Corporation* [1947] 2 All ER 680.

16 *Magill v Porter* [2001] UKHL 67 at para 103. See also *R (Costas Georgiou) v London Borough of Enfield* [2004] EWHC 779 (Admin) and *R (on the application of Island Farm Development Ltd) v Bridgend County Borough Council* [2006] EWHC 2189 (Admin).

Further procedure required

It is, of course, possible that, at this stage, the local review body decides it does not have enough information before it to determine the application that is the subject of the notice of review. In that event, further procedure may be required as set out in the next chapter. It is generally accepted, however, that the same members should then take part in any subsequent meetings of the local review body.

Chapter 7

Determination after Further Procedure

If the application that is the subject of the notice of review is not determined at the first meeting of the local review body, then a range of options for further procedure is available to the local review body as to how it will consider and determine that application. The Scottish Government's Directorate for Planning and Environmental Appeals ('DPEA') has published guidance – *Reporter Guidance Note 8: Further Procedure* – which sets out relevant factors to be considered in deciding what form of further procedure is appropriate.[1] The further procedures for both written submissions and holding any hearing session are initiated by the local review body issuing a 'procedure notice'.[2] Site inspections may be unaccompanied or accompanied. Further details about these matters and the consideration of new evidence are set out below.

Given the busy nature of any committee calendar, and the pressures on members and officers alike, it may be that nothing further will happen following the first local review body meeting at which the application that is subject to the notice of review is considered until the next scheduled local review body meeting. Nevertheless, efforts should be made, wherever possible, to move the case along to its conclusion as expeditiously as possible whether or not the case is a non-determination application to be concluded within the prescribed three-month period.

1 www.gov.scot/Resource/0045/00458560.pdf
2 2013 Regulations, reg 2.

Decision as to the procedure to be followed

Regulation 13 of the 2013 Regulations states:

'(1) Where the local review body do not determine the review without further procedure, the local review body may determine the manner in which the review is to be conducted and are to do so in accordance with this regulation.

(2) The local review body may determine at any stage of the review that further representations should be made or further information should be provided to enable them to determine the review.

(3) Where the local review body so determine, the review or a stage of the review is to be conducted by one of, or by a combination of, the procedures mentioned in paragraph (4).

(4) The procedures are—
(a) by means of written submission;
(b) by the holding of one or more hearing sessions; and
(c) by means of an inspection of the land to which the review relates.

(5) Where the local review body consider that such further representations should be made or information should be made available or provided by means of—
(a) written submissions, regulation 15 applies;
(b) a hearing session, the Hearing Session Rules apply; or
(c) an inspection of the land, regulation 16 applies.

(6) Notices given under regulation 15(1) or rule 1(1) of the Hearing Session Rules may be given separately or combined into a single notice.'

Decisions about further procedures

The notice of review will include a statement about what, if any, procedures (or combination of procedures) mentioned in regulation 13(4) of the 2013 Regulations the applicant considers appropriate for the conduct of the review.[3]

Regulation 13(2) of the 2013 Regulations states that the local review body may determine 'at any stage of the review' that

---

3 2013 Regulations, reg 9(3)(d).

further representations should be made or further information should be provided to enable it to determine the review. In most cases it will be clear from considering the papers, and possibly further debate at the first local review body meeting, whether there is a lack of information or a need for some form of clarity on particular points which would trigger further procedure. In that situation it is perfectly competent for the local review body to decide there and then on the further procedure that is needed.

Pre-examination meetings

However, in terms of regulation 14 of the 2013 Regulations, should it wish to do so the local review body can hold a meeting known as a 'pre-examination meeting' to consider 'the manner in which the review or any stage of the review is to be conducted with a view to securing that the review or any stage of the review is conducted efficiently and expeditiously'.

Regulation 14 then provides that the local review body requires to determine the date, time or place for the pre-examination meeting; give notice of it to persons entitled to appear at a hearing session or, in any other case, the applicant, the planning authority and any interested party.[4] The local review body must also determine the matters to be discussed, and the procedure to be followed, at such a pre-examination meeting.[5]

At first sight, this provision for a pre-examination meeting appears to be unnecessary. The local review body can decide what further procedure is to be adopted at its first meeting to consider the case that is the subject of the notice of review. Indeed, the provision mirrors those in the Town and Country Planning (Appeals) (Scotland) Regulations 2013[6] and appears to have simply been imported wholesale from those appeals regulations where, arguably, it is much more appropriate.

Where an appeal is being dealt with by a reporter, it is much more likely that a hearing session of some complexity and/or a mix

4 2013 Regulations, reg 14(2) and (3).
5 2013 Regulations, reg 14(4).
6 SSI 2013/156. See, in particular, reg 10.

of hearing sessions and written submissions might be necessary to allow the reporter, who may have no prior knowledge of the site at all, to have sufficient information to decide the appeal. This is much less likely to be the case with a local development being considered by a local review body.

Circular 5/2013: *Schemes of Delegation and Local Reviews* ('Circular 5/2013'), at paragraph 39, recognises that a pre-examination meeting 'will not be appropriate in every case' and stresses that 'a pre-examination meeting will not be necessary in all but the more complex cases'.[7] However, Circular 5/2013 suggests 'where, for example, there is a range of issues to be examined or more than one procedure is likely to be used to support the review process, such a meeting can clarify for the applicant and interested parties the procedures and their respective roles and help ensure the review is conducted efficiently and expeditiously'.

Circular 5/2013, unlike its predecessor Circular 7/2009: *Schemes of Delegations and Local Reviews*,[8] does not suggest that the pre-examination meeting could take place when the review body meets to consider whether it has sufficient information to enable it to determine the review. The risk in combining a pre-examination meeting with the first meeting of the review body is that of confusion both in the minds of the parties and the local review body itself. For instance, is it proceeding under regulation 14 of the 2013 Regulations and, if so, at what stage in the meeting?

Written submissions

Regulation 15 of the 2013 Regulations addresses the written submissions procedure. It states:

'(1) Where the local review body has determined that further representations should be made or further information should be provided by means of written submissions, the local review body may request such further representations or information and is to do so by giving written notice to that effect to—

7 www.gov.scot/Publications/2013/12/8902
8 At para 37.

(a) the applicant; and

(b) any other body or person from whom the local review body wishes to receive further representations or information.

(2) The procedure notice given under paragraph (1) is to—

(a) set out the matters on which such further representations or information is requested;

(b) specify the date by which such further representations or information are to be sent to the appointed person; and

(c) provide the name and address of any body or person to whom the procedure notice is given.

(3) Any further representations made or information provided in response to the procedure notice ("the procedure notice response") are to be sent to the local review body on or before the date specified for that purpose in the procedure notice and a copy of any procedure notice response is to be sent on or before that date to any other person or body to whom the procedure notice was given.

(4) Within a period of 14 days from receipt of a copy of the procedure notice response, any body or person to whom the procedure notice was given—

(a) may send comments to the local review body in reply to the procedure notice response; and

(b) must when doing so send a copy of such comments to any other person or body to whom the procedure notice was given.

(5) A copy of any procedure notice response or any comments required to be sent to a body or person under this regulation is to be sent to the body or person at the address provided for the body or person in the procedure notice.

(6) In this regulation "procedure notice response" has the meaning given in paragraph (3).'

Regulation 15 is relatively straightforward. The local review body decides it requires further representations or further information from certain people and issues a notice to them with a request for information by a specific date. Where more than one person is required to provide information, then each of them is to receive notification of the other's name and address so that their written submissions are then circulated by them to those other persons. This allows another 14-day period of comment.

It is not clear what happens if the written submissions are sent in outwith the date provided for, or if comments are received after the 14-day period specified in regulation 15(4) of the 2013 Regulations. Presumably it is at the discretion of the local review body to consider late submissions or comments although doing so could be seen to be technically in breach of the regulations.

Again, it is left at the discretion of the local review body as to what procedure then takes place. However, it is assumed that in almost every case the further written submissions and comments, if any, will be placed before the next available meeting of the local review body, on the understanding that this should provide sufficient information for the local review body to determine the case.

Hearing sessions and related rules

It is probable that, in most cases, it will be possible to decide the case on the basis of, at most, written submissions and a site inspection. The provisions about convening a hearing etc are likely to only be used sparingly, given the narrower spectrum of issues that are usually relevant in 'local development' planning applications. It should be remembered that any local review body hearing will take the form of a discussion led by the local review body. Further cross-examination can be allowed in a local review body hearing session. However, cross-examination is not permitted in an appeal hearing session held by one of the Scottish Ministers' reporters.[9]

However, a local review body may decide that it is necessary to convene a hearing so that issues set out in the notice of review and related documentation can be properly considered. If so, the local review body needs to consider, and specify, what it actually needs to have a hearing about. Only those matters set out in a 'procedure notice' issued by a local review body can be considered in any hearing sessions.

Some hearings will involve highly technical matters. It can be helpful for a local review body to have access to the advice of an

9 Compare 2013 Regulations, Sch 1, para 5(5) and Town and Country Planning (Appeals) (Scotland) Regulations 2013 (SSI 2013/156), Sch 1, para 5(5).

expert on such matters, rather than being asked to draw conclusions about conflicting technical expert evidence. In some instances it might be helpful for a local review body to receive expert advice regarding the scope of technical matters to be included in a 'procedure notice'. However, a local review body is only empowered to appoint an assessor to sit with the local review body 'at a hearing session' to advise it on such matters arising as it may specify. If such an appointment is made, the local review body must notify every person entitled to appear at the hearing session of the name of the assessor, and of the matters on which the assessor is to advise the local review body. Where an assessor has been appointed, the assessor may (and if so required by the local review body must), after the close of the hearing session, make a report in writing to the local review body in respect of the matters on which the assessor was appointed to advise.[10]

Conducting a hearing

The courts have considered the role of an inspector in a hearing. They have summarised the role of the inspector at a hearing as:

- having responsibility for bringing out such evidence as is required in order to decide the main issues that the inspector has identified;
- providing, if necessary, the parties with an opportunity to introduce evidence or documents or other information into the hearing which had not previously been referred to;
- obtaining and adducing any relevant or significant evidence;
- permitting, where appropriate, cross-examination of all those present or of a particular witness or witnesses or, in an extreme case, to abandon the hearing so as to allow the appeal to be determined as an inquiry; and
- having the overriding objective of conducting the hearing fairly,[11] expeditiously and economically so as to determine the appeal in a single hearing lasting no more than about one day

10 2013 Regulations, reg 21 – referred to in Chapter 6.
11 See, eg, *Dyason v Secretary of State for the Environment Transport and the Regions* [1998] JPL 778.

having addressed the main issues and having given the applicant and the planning authority a reasonable opportunity of explaining their respective points of view in a non-technical environment.[12]

The court's summary of the inquisitorial nature of a hearing can be applied with appropriate modifications. For instance, it is outwith the powers of a local review body to hold an inquiry. Only hearing sessions may be held by a local review body.

The 'Hearing Session Rules' are set out in Schedule 1 to the 2013 Regulations. They do not cover every aspect of the procedure. Planning authorities should consider whether they should standardise hearings by for instance having supplementary rules which set out, for example, the order in which matters are to be considered at the hearing session, the order in which people entitled to appear at the hearing session are to be heard and time limits, if any, for presentations made by the applicant or an interested party. A local review body hearing must be held in public.[13] The other key provisions of the Hearing Rules are summarised below.

Notice about hearing session and specified matters

Where the local review body has determined that a hearing session should be held it must give written notice (a 'procedure notice') to that effect to the applicant; any interested party who made representations in relation to specified matters set out in the procedure notice; and any other body or person from whom the local review body wishes to receive further representations or to provide further information on specified matters at a hearing session. The notice given by the local review body must specify the matters to be considered at the hearing session and only specified matters are to be considered at the hearing session. A person given notice by the local review body and who intends to appear at the hearing session must within 14 days of the date of such notice inform the local review body in writing of that intention.

---

12 *AZ v Secretary of State for Communities and Local Government and Another* [2012] EWHC 3660 (Admin) at paras [105]–[107].
13 2013 Regulations, reg 7.

Appearances at hearing session

The persons entitled to appear at a hearing session are the applicant and any other person who, in response to a procedure notice, has informed the local review body in writing within 14 days of the date of the procedure notice of their intention to appear at the hearing session.

Date and notification of hearing session

The date, time and place at which the hearing session is to be held is to be determined (and may subsequently be varied) by the local review body. The local review body is to give to those persons entitled to appear at the hearing session such notice of the date, time and place fixed for the holding of a hearing session (and any subsequent variation thereof) as may appear to the local review body to be reasonable in the circumstances.

Service of hearing statements and documents

If required to do so by notice given by the local review body, a person entitled to appear at the hearing session must, by such date as is specified in the notice, send to the local review body and to such other persons entitled to appear at the hearing session as the local review body may specify in the notice:

- 'a hearing statement' (that is a written statement which fully sets out the case relating to the specified matters which a person proposes to put forward at a hearing session; a list of documents (if any) which the person putting forward the case intends to refer to or rely on; and a list of any other persons who are to speak at the hearing session in respect of the case, any matters which such persons are particularly to address and any relevant qualifications of such persons to do so); and
- where that person intends to refer to or rely on any documents when presenting their case a list of all such documents and a copy of every document (or the relevant part of a document) on that list which is not already available for inspection in terms of the relevant legislation.

The planning authority is, until such time as the review is determined, to afford to any person who so requests a reasonable opportunity to inspect and, where practicable, take copies of any hearing statement or other document (or any part thereof) which, or a copy of which, has been sent to the local review body.

Any person who has served a hearing statement must when required by notice in writing from the local review body provide such further information about the matters contained in the statement as the local review body may specify; and at the same time send a copy of such further information to any other person on whom the hearing statement has been served.

Procedure at a local review body hearing

Except as otherwise provided in the Hearing Session Rules, the procedure at a hearing shall be as the local review body determines.

Having considered any submission by the persons entitled to appear at the hearing session the local review body is to state at or before the commencement of the hearing session the procedure which it proposes to adopt. A local review body has, in particular, to state the order in which:

- the specified matters are to be considered at the hearing session; and
- the persons entitled to appear at the hearing session are to be heard in relation to a specified matter (a different order may be chosen for different specified matters).

Any person entitled to appear at the hearing may do so on that person's own behalf or be represented by another person. Where there are two or more persons having a similar interest in the issues being considered at the hearing session, the local review body may allow one or more persons to appear on behalf of some or all of any persons so interested. The local review body may proceed with a hearing session in the absence of any person entitled to appear at the hearing session. However, the local review body needs to consider an adjournment if a person is unable to attend the hearing.[14]

A hearing shall take the form of a discussion led by the local review body. Cross-examination is not permitted unless the local review body considers that cross-examination is required to ensure a thorough examination of the issues.[15]

In general a person entitled to appear at a local review body hearing session is entitled to call evidence. However, the local review body may refuse to permit

- the giving or production of evidence;
- the cross-examination of persons giving evidence; or
- the presentation of any other matter

which it considers is irrelevant or repetitious.

The local review body may from time to time adjourn the hearing session. If the date, time and place of the adjourned hearing session are announced before the adjournment, no further notice is required. Otherwise such notice as may appear to the local review body to be reasonable in the circumstances must be given of the date, time and place of the adjourned hearing session to the persons entitled to appear at the hearing session.

Legal advice at a local review body hearing

Circular 5/2013 states that planning authorities will want to ensure that the local review body is supported by appropriate administrative and legal advice to ensure that members are guided on the review process. A legal adviser may be called upon to provide advice during a hearing. The best practice would be:

- provisional legal advice is given to the local review body in public;

---

14 *West Lancashire District Council v Secretary of State for the Environment, Transport and the Regions* [1999] JPL 890.

15 2013 Regulations, Sch 1 para 5(5). This can be contrasted with Town and Country Planning (Appeals) (Scotland) Regulations 2013 (SSI 2013/156) which provides that cross-examination is not permitted at hearing sessions.

- the parties are afforded an opportunity to comment upon the legal advice given; and
- the legal adviser should then state in public whether the provisional advice is confirmed or is varied, and if it is varied in what respect, before the local review body decides to act upon the legal advice given to it.[16]

Site inspection

A common piece of further procedure is a site inspection. Often, no matter how many visual representations of the site have been made available to the local review body, there is no substitute for physically seeing the site and its inter-relationship with other buildings, road access and so on. This is particularly the case if visual or other amenity issues are to the fore or road safety aspects of the development being serviced by a substandard access point.

Regulation 16 of the 2013 Regulations provides that the local review body may at any time make either an unaccompanied inspection or an accompanied inspection of the land to which the notice of review relates. The provisions of this regulation are similar to those in regulation 12 of the Town and Country Planning (Appeals) (Scotland) Regulations 2013. Standing that similarity, local review bodies may wish to have regard to the DPEA's *Reporter Guidance Note 6: Site inspections (accompanied or unaccompanied)*.[17] The local review body may also wish to have regard to the Local Review Body Forum's best practice guidance note *Site inspections undertaken by Local Review Bodies*.[18]

Where the local review body intends to make an unaccompanied site inspection, it must inform the applicant that it proposes to do so.[19]

An accompanied inspection would consist of the site inspection

16 *Clark v Kelly* [2003] UKPC D1 and 2003 SLT 308 at para [69].
17 www.gov.scot/Resource/0042/00426746.pdf
18 www.gov.scot/Resource/0038/00389406.pdf
19 2013 Regulations, reg 16(2).

taking place with the applicant and any interested party. The local review body must give notice of the date and time of the accompanied inspection.[20]

Regulation 16(4) of the 2013 Regulations provides that the local review body is not bound to defer a site inspection if any person to whom notice was given is not present at the time appointed. However if the inspection is for instance carried out in the applicant's absence there may be a perception of injustice.[21]

Planning authorities are likely to have established procedures for 'site visits' in relation to planning permission applications which are to be determined by committee. These procedures might be usefully adapted to site inspections by local review bodies. However, officers accompanying members of the local review body should bear in mind that a certain amount of formality needs to be observed during site inspections. Whether accompanied or unaccompanied, interaction between members and applicants, objectors and agents should be kept to a minimum.

Where a site inspection is deemed necessary, all members taking part in the final decision should have attended the inspection.

New evidence after the conclusion of further procedure

Regulation 17 of the 2013 Regulations provides that if, after the conclusion of any further procedure conducted by virtue of regulation 13 of the 2013 Regulations, the local review body proposes to take into consideration any new evidence which is material to the determination of the review, then the applicant and any other 'relevant party' need to be afforded an opportunity to make representations on such new evidence. This provision only applies where the new evidence relates either to matters which were specified in a procedure notice issued under the Hearing Session Rules and considered at a hearing session or to matters in respect of which further

20 2013 Regulations, reg 16(3).
21 See, eg, *R (on the application of Tait) v Secretary of State for Communities and Local Government* [2012] EWHC 643 (Admin).

written representations or information were sought by a procedure notice under regulation 15 of the 2013 Regulations.[22]

Right of appeal where local review body has failed to determine application timeously

The right of appeal to the Scottish Ministers under section 43A(17) of the 1997 Act is referred to in Chapter 9. If the case under review is not taken away from the local review body by an appeal to the Scottish Ministers or otherwise, the local review body has a continuing obligation to determine the 'local development' planning application which is the subject of the notice of review (see Chapter 4).

22 2013 Regulations, reg 17(2).

Chapter 8

Decisions of Appointed Officers and Local Review Body Decision Notices

In the main the previous chapters have addressed the relevant law about processes leading to a determination of the relevant 'local development' planning application. Clearly all planning authorities should aim to get the decision right first time.

In 2010 the Scottish Government published a useful guide *Right first time: A practical guide for public authorities in Scotland to decision-making and the law.*[1] That guide refers to various legal principles in decision-taking and draws upon planning cases and relevant court decisions. It may be a helpful tool for both planning authority officers and members of a local review body.

Planning authorities may also wish to give consideration to ensuring that the reports on handling prepared by their officers reflect the requirements of a local review body decision notice. Such an approach may expedite decisions as it would allow a local review body to consider, and if appropriate, for instance, to adopt the findings and reasoning of the planning authority officer in the local review body's decision notice.

In this chapter we consider:

- how an appointed officer and a local review body ought to determine an application for planning permission;
- an appointed officer's report on handling and a local review body's decision notice (including relevant common law requirements for a decision notice); and

---

1 www.gov.scot/Publications/2010/02/23134246/0

- issuing a local review body notice of intended decision and a local review body decision notice.

Determining an application for planning permission

Applications for planning permissions have to be determined in accordance with section 37(2) and section 25 of the 1997 Act. The courts have referred to section 25 of the 1997 Act introducing 'a priority to be given to the development plan in the determination of planning matters'. The courts have set out the proper approach for planning authorities determining such applications, namely the decision-maker should:

- identify the provisions of the development plan which are relevant to the determination of the application being considered;
- properly interpret those provisions – this is a matter of law (policies should be interpreted objectively in accordance with the language used, read as always in its proper context but should not be construed as if they were statutory or contractual provisions);
- consider whether or not the proposal accords with the development plan;
- identify and consider relevant material considerations both for and against the proposal; and
- assess whether, on balance, those considerations warrant the grant of planning permission for a proposed development although it is contrary to the development plan or the refusal of planning permission for a proposed development albeit that it accords with the development plan.[2]

The planning authority must take its decision in light of the provisions of the development plan and material considerations at the

---

2 See the 1997 Act, s 25 and, eg, *City of Edinburgh Council v Secretary of State for Scotland* [1997] UKHL 38, *Tesco Stores Ltd v Dundee City Council* [2012] UKSC 13 and *R (on the application of Cherkley Campaign Ltd) v Mole Valley District Council* [2014] EWCA Civ 567.

date of the decision (not at some earlier date such as the date of conclusion of a local review body hearing).[3]

The development plan

The development plan for a proposed development site will comprise:

- in the four city regions of Aberdeen (Aberdeen City and Shire), Dundee (TAYplan), Edinburgh (SESplan) and Glasgow (Glasgow and the Clyde Valley)[4] the relevant strategic development plan, the relevant local development plan (failing which the extant adopted local plan) and any supplementary guidance issued under section 22 of the 1997 Act; and
- outwith the four city regions of Aberdeen, Dundee, Edinburgh and Glasgow, the relevant local development plan (failing which the extant adopted local plan) and any supplementary guidance issued under section 22 of the 1997 Act.

A decision-maker must interpret policy properly. Policy statements should be interpreted objectively in accordance with the language used, read as always in its proper context. The interpretation of policy is a matter of law. An error by a planning authority in interpreting its policies would be the basis for a successful challenge to a decision based on a misinterpretation of policy and where there was a real possibility that its determination might otherwise have been different.[5]

Policy statements should not be construed as if they were statutory or contractual provisions. Although a development plan has a legal status and legal effects, it is not analogous in its nature or purpose to a statute or a contract. Development plans are full of broad statements of policy, many of which may be mutually irreconcilable, so that in a particular case one must give way to another. In addition, many of the provisions of development plans

---

3 See, eg, *Oxford Diocesan Board of Finance v Secretary of State for Communities and Local Government* [2013] EWHC 802 (Admin).
4 Scottish Government Circular 1/2013: *Strategic Development Plan Areas.*
5 *Tesco Stores Ltd v Dundee City Council* [2012] UKSC 13 at [18].

are framed in language whose application to a given set of facts requires the exercise of judgment. Such matters fall within the jurisdiction of planning authorities, and their exercise of their judgment can only be challenged on the ground that it is irrational or perverse. Nevertheless, planning authorities do not live in the world of Humpty Dumpty: they cannot make the development plan mean whatever they would like it to mean.[6]

Material considerations

What is a material consideration is a question of law. Courts must be concerned only with the legality of the decision-making process not with the planning merits of the decision. The weight to be given to any material consideration is a question of planning judgment. Matters of planning judgment are the exclusive province of the planning authority – including the appointed officer or the local review body as the case may be.[7]

Material considerations should:

- serve or be related to the purpose of planning and should therefore relate to the development and use of land; and
- fairly and reasonably relate to the particular application being considered.

The range of considerations which might be considered to be material (ie relevant) in planning terms is very wide and can only be determined in the context of the particular case under consideration. Examples of material considerations include:

- UK Government policies on reserved matters and Scottish Government policies on devolved matters;
- *Scottish Planning Policy*;[8] *Creating Places*[9] and *Designing Streets*;[10]
- a National Park Plan;

---

6   *Tesco Stores Ltd v Dundee City Council* at [19] and *Tesco Stores Ltd v Secretary of State for the Environment* [1995] UKHL 22.

7   *Tesco Stores Ltd v Secretary of State for the Environment* at [56] and [57].

8   www.gov.scot/Publications/2014/06/5823

9   www.gov.scot/Publications/2013/06/9811/0

10 www.gov.scot/Publications/2010/03/22120652/0

- a proposed strategic development plan, local development plan or supplementary guidance made under section 22 of the 1997 Act;
- guidance adopted by a strategic development plan authority or a planning authority that is not supplementary guidance adopted under section 22 of the 1997 Act;
- the design of the proposed development and its relationship to its surroundings;
- views of statutory or other consultees about the proposed development;
- risk of creating a precedent for further development;[11] and
- public objections or support founded on relevant planning grounds.[12]

Determining a notice of review

In Chapter 4 we considered the content of a notice of review. The prohibition about raising new matters or issues is addressed in Chapter 3. A local review body's ability to consider new material about the issues raised before the appointed officer's decision and to consider new evidence after the conclusion of further procedure are set out in Chapters 3 and 7 respectively. The requirement that a local review body must consider, and record, details of the provisions of the development plan and other material considerations to which it had regard in determining the application is discussed in Chapter 3.

Report on handling and local review body decision notice

The local review body in arriving at its decision will consider the 'review documents' including any related 'report on handling' pre-

---

11 See, eg, *R (on the application of Holder) v Gedling Borough Council* [2014] EWCA Civ 599.

12 For more detail about material considerations see, eg Circular 3/2013: *Development Management Procedures*, Annex A and R McMaster, A Prior and J Watchman, *Scottish Planning Law* (3rd edn, 2013) ch 6.

pared by an appointed officer. A local review body's decision notice must include:

- the terms on which the planning authority through its local review body has decided the case reviewed;
- the reasons for the decision; and
- other prescribed matters including details of the provisions of the development plan and any other material considerations to which the local review body had regard in determining the application.[13]

A relevant report on handling may form part of the reasons on which a local review body bases its decision. It has been said that:

- there will inevitably be aspects of a case in respect of which similar views are reached between the appointed officer at first instance and the local review body and other aspects where differing views are reached;
- it would be pedantic to require a local review body to restate the aspects of the appointed person's decision which are accepted; and
- all that is necessary, in the relevant statutory context, is that where the local review body's decision is different from that of the appointed person, the local review body should make plain its reasons for reaching a different decision.[14]

As noted above it would appear to assist a local review body if the appointed person's report on handling reflects the requirements for a local review body decision notice.

Statutory requirements for a local review body's decision notice

In the case of an application for planning permission a local review body's decision notice must in addition to the matters required by section 43A(12)(a) of the 1997 Act:

---

13 1997 Act, s 43A(12) and 2013 Regulations, reg 22.
14 *Carroll v Scottish Borders Council* [2014] CSOH 6 at [44] and [46].

- include the reference number of the application;
- include a description of the location of the proposed development including, where applicable, a postal address;
- include a description of the proposed development (including identification of the plans and drawings showing the proposed development) for which planning permission has been granted, or as the case may be, refused;
- include a description of any variation made to the application in accordance with section 32A(a) of the 1997 Act;
- specify any conditions to which the decision is subject;
- include a statement as to the effect of section 58(2) or 59(4) of the 1997 Act, as the case may be, or where the planning authority have made a direction under section 58(2) or 59(5) of the 1997 Act, give details of that direction;
- if any obligation is to be entered into under section 75 of the 1997 Act in connection with the application, state where the terms of such obligation or a summary of such terms may be inspected; and
- include details of the provisions of the development plan and any other material considerations to which the local review body had regard in determining the application.[15]

In the case of an application for consent, agreement or approval required by condition imposed on a grant of planning permission a local review body's decision notice must include:

- a description of the matter in respect of which approval, consent or agreement has been granted or, as the case may be, refused;
- the reference number of the application; and
- the reference number of the application for the planning permission in respect of which the condition in question was imposed.[16]

---

15 2013 Regulations, reg 22(2)(a). The Town and Country Planning (Appeals) (Scotland) Regulations 2013 (SSI 2013/156) do not impose similar requirements upon the Scottish Ministers' reporters.

16 2013 Regulations, reg 22(2)(b).

A local review body's decision notice must in the case of refusal or approval subject to conditions be accompanied by a notification in the terms set out in Schedule 2 to the 2013 Regulations (about statutory application under sections 237 and 239 of the 1997 Act to the Court of Session and a purchase notice under Part V of the 1997 Act).[17]

The Scottish Government's 2008 consultation draft of relevant legislation proposed that a local review body's decision notice must also contain provisions such as:

- a statement of the number of representations made in respect of the application and a summary of the main issues raised by such representations;
- details of the authorities and persons consulted by the planning authority in respect of the application and a summary of the responses made by such authorities or persons;
- a statement as to whether:
  - an appropriate assessment under the Conservation (Natural Habitats &c) Regulations 1994 was carried out in respect of the proposed development;
  - a design and access statement was submitted in respect of the proposed development; or
  - any report on the impact or potential impact of the proposed development (for example the retail impact, transport impact, noise impact or risk of flooding) was submitted in connection with the application, and where such a statement or report was submitted or such assessment carried out, a summary of the main issues raised by such statement, report or assessment; and
  - particulars of any direction given under the 1997 Act or relevant regulations in respect of the application.[18]

However, the above requirements were not subsequently included in the relevant regulations.

17 2013 Regulations, reg 22(3).
18 www.gov.scot/Publications/2008/02/13104117/14

Common law requirements of a local review body decision notice

A local review body must give adequate reasons for its decisions. The relevant legal principles for a reasoned planning decision have been summarised as follows:

'The reasons for a decision must be intelligible and they must be adequate. They must enable the reader to understand why the matter was decided as it was and what conclusions were reached on the principal important controversial issues, disclosing how any issue of law or fact was resolved. Reasons can be briefly stated, the degree of particularity required depending entirely on the nature of the issues falling for decision. The reasoning must not give rise to a substantial doubt as to whether the decision-maker erred in law, for example by misunderstanding some relevant policy or some other important matter or by failing to reach a rational decision on relevant grounds. But such adverse inference will not readily be drawn. The reasons need refer only to the main issues in the dispute, not to every material consideration. They should enable disappointed developers to assess their prospects of obtaining some alternative development permission, or, as the case may be, their unsuccessful opponents to understand how the policy or approach underlying the grant of permission may impact upon future such applications. Decision letters must be read in a straightforward manner, recognising that they are addressed to parties well aware of the issues involved and the arguments advanced. A reasons challenge will only succeed if the party aggrieved can satisfy the court that he has genuinely been substantially prejudiced by the failure to provide an adequately reasoned decision.'[19]

The adequacy of reasons for a planning decision has also been considered by the UK Supreme Court.[20] It stated that:

'In considering the adequacy of the reasons given for a decision, it is necessary to take account of a number of matters, including the nature of the decision in question, the context in which it has been

19 *South Bucks District Council v Porter* [2004] UKHL 33 at para [36]. See also Local Review Body Forum guidance note: *Decision Notices* — www.gov.scot/Resource/0038/00389408.pdf
20 *Uprichard v Scottish Ministers* [2013] UKSC 21.

made, the purpose for which the reasons are provided and the context in which they are given.

'It is in addition important to maintain a sense of proportion when considering the duty to give reasons, and not to impose on decision-makers a burden which is unreasonable having regard to the purpose intended to be served.'

Judicial consideration of a local review body decision notice

As noted above the courts have said that it is necessary, within the statutory structure of review for local developments, that the decision of a local review body should make plain what are the reasons for reaching a different decision from that of the planning authority's appointed officer.[21]

Issue of notice of intention instead of a decision notice

In most instances where the local review body decides to grant the application that is the subject of a notice of review, the grant will either be unconditional or subject to conditions.[22]

There may be cases where it is necessary for a local review body to defer issuing its decision notice and in these instances it may be that the local review body will wish to issue a notice of its intended decision. These cases are if:

- a direction has been issued by the Scottish Ministers not to issue planning permission;
- the application being considered has to be notified to the Scottish Ministers under the Town and Country Planning (Notification of Applications) (Scotland) Direction 2009 – which is set out in Circular 3/2009: *Notification of Planning Applications*; or
- the local review body has resolved to grant planning per-

21 *Carroll v Scottish Borders Council* [2014] CSOH 6 at para [46].
22 Circular 4/1998: *The Use of Conditions in Planning Permission* and Circular 3/2012: *Planning Obligations and Good Neighbour Agreements*.

mission subject to the conclusion of a legal agreement or a planning obligation – see Circular 3/2012: *Planning Obligations and Good Neighbour Agreements*.

Issuing a local review body decision notice

In all instances (in particular those cases which require notification of the application to the Scottish Ministers or the conclusion of a planning obligation or other legal agreement) there will be a delay between the decision taken at the meeting of the local review body and the issue of its decision notice.

Care should be taken to ensure that there are no outstanding matters that require attention prior to issuing the local review body's decision notice.[23] In particular, before a local review body decision is issued consideration ought to be given to any change in circumstances since the date of the decision of the local review body to ascertain whether:

- it is necessary to refer the application back to the local review body to reconsider its decision in light of the change of circumstances in the intervening period;[24] and
- the decision notice can properly be issued.

Reasoned decisions must be issued within time limits stipulated in legislation such as the Civic Government (Scotland) Act 1982 and the Licensing (Scotland) Act 2005.[25] However, there is no legislative time limit for the issue of a local review body decision notice.

The COSLA/Improvement Service guidance *Local Review Bodies* states that a local review body decision notice:

23 See, eg, *R (on the application of Timothy Carroll) v South Somerset District Council* [2008] EWHC 104 (Admin).

24 See, eg, *R (on the application of Kides) v South Cambridgeshire District Council* [2002] EWCA Civ 1370 and *R (on the application of Marton-cum-Grafton Parish Council) v North Yorkshire County Council* [2013] EWHC 2406 (Admin).

25 Within 10 days of being required to do so under the Civic Government (Scotland) Act 1982 and within 14 days of being required to do so under the Licensing (Procedure) (Scotland) Regulations 2007 (SSI 2007/453) respectively.

- should be issued within a reasonable period of the local review body's decision;[26] and
- planning authorities (acting through their local review bodies) should normally aim to issue decision notices within 21 days (of the meeting at which the decision is taken) except in the most complex cases.

The 2013–14 planning statistics published by the Scottish Government indicate that across Scotland the average timetable for local review bodies to determine a case is almost 13 weeks. However, performance varies markedly across Scotland with some local review bodies determining applications on average after five weeks and at the opposite end of the spectrum after 31 weeks.

If the local review body has not lost jurisdiction to determine the application that is the subject of the notice of review by an appeal to the Scottish Ministers under section 43A(17) of the 1997 Act or otherwise, the local review body has a continuing obligation to take a decision on the application that is subject to a notice of review.[27]

---

26 See *Lafarge Redland Aggregates Ltd v Scottish Ministers* 2000 SLT 1361.
27 See Chapter 4.

Chapter 9

Planning Permission Appeals, Statutory Applications, Petitions for Judicial Review and Complaints

In many instances in the development management process there will be someone who is disappointed. It may be the applicant (for instance, because the planning authority is taking too long to determine the application or because the application has been refused) or an 'interested party' (for example, a person who has objected to an application for planning permission which was subsequently granted by the planning authority). Further questions may arise about the conduct of a local review body member, about the conduct of a person advising a local review body or about the lawfulness of the decision of the local review body.[1]

In this chapter we consider:

- the right of appeal to the Scottish Ministers where there are two deemed refusals, including a deemed refusal by a local review body of an application for planning permission for a 'local development' or any application for consent, agreement or approval required by a condition imposed on a grant of planning permission for such development;
- scrutiny by the Court of Session of a statutory application challenging the legality of any decision (other than a deemed

---

1 For instance, in *Carroll v Scottish Borders Council* [2014] CSOH 6 an objector to the planning application made a statutory application to the Court of Session on various legal grounds (including failure to properly interpret policy and *Wednesbury* unreasonableness) regarding a decision by the Scottish Borders Council (through its local review body), reversing the decision of its appointed officer, to grant planning permission for the erection of wind turbines.

refusal decision) of a local review body in a review conducted by it or a petition for judicial review at common law challenging the legality of an act, decision or omission of a local review body; and

- potential avenues for complaints to a variety of bodies including: complaints to a local authority's Monitoring Officer; complaints about councillors to the Commissioner for Ethical Standards in Public Life in Scotland and the Standards Commission for Scotland; complaints about members of the Royal Town Planning Institute; complaints about lawyers to the Scottish Legal Complaints Commission; and complaints to the Scottish Public Services Ombudsman about planning authorities (including their local review bodies).

Right of appeal to the Scottish Ministers

In a small number of cases there will be a right of appeal to the Scottish Ministers. This right arises where there have been two deemed refusals of an application for planning permission, or for consent agreement or approval required by a condition imposed on a grant of planning permission, for a 'local development'. First the relevant application must be capable of being determined by a person appointed by virtue of a scheme of delegation made under section 43(1) of the 1997 Act, and there has been a deemed refusal by the appointed person[2] and then there has been a deemed refusal by a local review body.[3]

That right of appeal to the Scottish Ministers exists where:

- the appointed person has failed to determine the application within the prescribed period – four months after the validation date of an application for planning permission for 'EIA

---

2 1997 Act, s 43A(8)(c) (as amended from 2 February 2013 by Public Services Reform (Planning) (Local Review Procedure) (Scotland) Order 2013 (SSI 2013/24)), s 43A(9) of the 1997 Act and 2013 Regulations, reg 8(2).
3 1997 Act, s 43A(17).

development'[4] and in any other case two months after the validation date of the relevant application;[5] or such extended period as agreed upon in writing by the applicant and the appointed person before the expiry of that period;[6]

- a requirement to review was made within the period of three months beginning with the date of expiry of the period allowed for the appointed person's determination of the application for planning permission;[7] and
- the local review body has not conducted the review within three months beginning on the date when the requirement to review was made.[8]

If the applicant does not appeal to the Scottish Ministers the local review body is required to reach its decision within a reasonable time.[9]

Access to the Court of Session

Any court proceedings must be raised in the Court of Session.

---

4 That is development, other than development in respect of which the Scottish Ministers have made a direction that the Town and Country Planning (Environmental Impact Assessment) (Scotland) Regulations 2011 (SSI 2011/139) ('the 2011 Regulations') will not apply to a particular proposed development; which development is either of a description mentioned (a) in Sch 1 to the 2011 Regulations; or (b) in column 1 of Sch 2 to the 2011 Regulations where (i) any part of that development is to be carried out in a 'sensitive area'; or (ii) any applicable threshold or criterion in the corresponding part of column 2 of the table in Sch 2 is respectively exceeded or met in relation to that development which development is likely to have significant effects on the environment by virtue of factors such as its nature, size or location.

5 1997 Act, s 43A(8)(c) and 2013 Regulations, reg 8(2).

6 1997 Act, s 43A(8)(c) as amended by Public Services Reform (Planning) (Local Review Procedure) (Scotland) Order 2013 (SSI 2013/24) and, eg *Vattenfall Wind Power Ltd v Scottish Ministers* [2009] CSIH 27.

7 1997 Act, s 43A(8)(c) and s 43A(9) and 2013 Regulations, reg 9.

8 1997 Act, s 43A(17) and 2013 Regulations, reg 8(3).

9 *Lafarge Redland Aggregates Ltd v Scottish Ministers* 2000 SLT 1361. See also *Vattenfall Wind Power Ltd v Scottish Ministers*.

Legal costs of litigation

The cost of pursuing court proceedings is a fundamental issue that must be considered by any person thinking of commencing court proceedings.

In general, in court proceedings awards of expenses follow success. So the court will order that a successful party's court expenses are met by any unsuccessful party. However, court expenses do not reflect full legal costs. So at best a person who is successful might have to pay around 40 per cent of their legal costs. However, a person should consider the worst case scenario of being unsuccessful and in turn meeting their own legal costs and in addition paying about 60 per cent of the costs of any successful opponent(s). This may mean that a decision is taken not to commence court proceedings.

Protective expenses orders

More recently the courts have made protective expenses orders (know as protective costs orders south of the border). These regulate the liability to pay court expenses. An order might be sought at common law[10] or under Court of Session Rule 58A (Protective Expenses Orders in Environmental Appeals and Judicial Reviews). It should be noted that this rule applies to both applications to the court's supervisory jurisdiction (judicial review) and to statutory applications.[11] In the case of rule 58A applications the applicant must be an individual or a non-governmental organisation promoting environmental protection and a protective expenses order may limit

---

10 Application to be considered under the principles set out in *R (Corner House Research) v Secretary of State for Trade and Industry* [2005] EWCA Civ 192. See, eg, *McGinty v Scottish Ministers* [2010] CSOH 5; *Road Sense v Scottish Ministers* [2011] CSOH 10 and *Newton Mearns Residents Flood Prevention Group for Cheviot Drive v East Renfrewshire Council* [2013] CSIH 70.

11 See, eg, *Carroll v Scottish Borders Council* [2014] CSOH 30; *Petition of Friends of Loch Etive* [2014] CSOH 116; and *John Muir Trust v Scottish Ministers* [2014] CSOH 172A.

- the applicant's liability in expenses to the respondent to the sum of £5,000 (which may be reduced in the particular circumstances of a case); and
- the respondent's liability in expenses to the applicant to the sum of £30,000 (which may be increased in the particular circumstances of the case)

with the objective of a protective expenses order being to ensure that court proceedings are not prohibitively expensive for the applicant.[12]

The Court of Session has provided guidance about the operation of rule 58A in practice, in particular in its decision in *Carroll v Scottish Borders Council*.[13]

In considering whether proceedings are prohibitively expensive for a non-governmental organisation ('NGO') the court must consider, as far as it can on the information available, the nature and extent of the work of the NGO and proceed on the basis that the NGO should be able to continue with its activities as long as it does so in good faith and not extravagantly or imprudently.[14]

Jurisdiction of the courts and the court's discretion to make orders

The jurisdiction of the courts is confined to legal issues, a long-held principle affirmed by the House of Lords:

'[It is] a fundamental principle of British planning law . . . that the courts are concerned only with the legality of the decision-making process and not with the merits of the decision. If there is one principle of planning law more firmly settled than any other, it is that

12 Act of Sederunt (Rules of the Court of Session 1994) 1994 (SI 1994/1443) as amended and see www.scotcourts.gov.uk/rules-and-practice/rules-of-court/court-of-session-rules
13 [2014] CSOH 30 at para [25] and paragraphs referred to therein.
14 *John Muir Trust v Scottish Ministers* [2014] CSOH 172A.

matters of planning judgment are within the exclusive province of the local planning authority or the Secretary of State.'[15]

So the Court of Session, in considering either a statutory application or a petition for judicial review:

- will not concern itself with the planning merits of the decision, for example the significance or otherwise of the impact of a proposed development on the environment;
- will be concerned about the legal validity or *vires* of the act, decision or omission that is before it; and
- cannot intervene unless and to the extent a planning authority exceeds its jurisdiction or fails to exercise its jurisdiction in a proper manner.

The possible benefits of pursuing court proceedings (including what orders a court might make) are also a significant issue that must be considered by any person thinking of commencing court proceedings.

Discretion to quash unlawful act, decision or omission

The orders that the Court of Session may make are detailed below. However, it is important to note that the court has discretion about the orders that it makes. For instance, if the court decides that the decision of the local review body is legally flawed it does not automatically follow that the court will quash the decision and the matters will be remitted back to the local review body to re-determine the application in light of the court's opinion and any change of circumstances in the intervening period since the decision was made.[16]

The risks are that:

- the court decides not to quash the decision and the decision therefore stands; or

15 *Tesco Stores Ltd v Secretary of State for the Environment* [1995] UKHL 22 at para 57, per Lord Hoffmann. The final sentence of this passage was quoted with approval, also in the House of Lords, in *City of Edinburgh Council v Secretary of State for Scotland and Others* [1997] UKHL 38, per Lord Clyde.

16 See, eg, *R (on the application of Burridge) v Breckland District Council* [2013] EWCA Civ 228.

- when the local review body re-determines the application it makes the same decision only this time it makes a legally sustainable decision.

One possible, even likely, outcome is that the pending court proceedings create a hiatus in a project's progress because the development approved by the local review body is not advanced further due to the uncertainties caused by the pending court proceedings.

Statutory application to the Court of Session

If any person is aggrieved by the action on the part of a planning authority in any decision or determination (other than a deemed decision) in a review conducted by such an authority by virtue of section 43A(8) of the 1997 Act and wishes to question the validity of that action on the grounds:

- that the action is not within the powers of the 1997 Act; or
- that any of the relevant requirements have not been complied with in relation to that action;

such a person may make an application to the Court of Session to challenge any such local review body decision or determination (other than a deemed decision) in a review conducted by it[17] within six weeks from the date on which the action is taken.[18]

Person aggrieved

The applicant must be a 'person aggrieved'[19] by the action of the local review body if that person is to qualify as having title to sue. In general what is required is some connection with the decision or determination through participation in the planning process that pre-dates it. However, in the circumstances of the particular case there may be an exception to that principle.[20]

---

17 1997 Act, ss 47(1A), 237(3A) and 239(4).
18 1997 Act, s 239(3).
19 See E Young, '"Aggrieved Persons" in Planning Law' 1993 SLT 43.
20 See, eg, *Cumming v Secretary of State for Scotland* 1993 SLT 228.

In the case of a decision by a local review body both the applicant for planning permission etc considered by the local review body and any 'interested party'[21] (generally any person from whom the planning authority received representations about the application) whose representations have not been withdrawn would be a 'person aggrieved'.

Grounds for statutory application

The grounds for the statutory application are generally regarded as encompassing the same grounds that are available in a petition for judicial review at common law challenging acts, decisions or omissions of a planning authority.

The principal grounds for a statutory application are:

- basing a decision on a material error of law going to the root of the question for determination;
- taking into account irrelevant considerations or failing to take into account relevant considerations;
- having no proper factual basis, where one is required to support a decision;
- unreasonableness, in the sense that no reasonable authority could have so acted;
- breach of natural justice, or of the duty to act fairly; or
- breach of a statutory requirement in the 1997 Act or related rules, where the effect of the breach is substantial rather than trivial.[22]

Court orders including order to quash decision

The Court of Session:

- may by interim order suspend the operation of the action in

---

21 2013 Regulations, reg 2.

22 See, eg, *Wordie Property Co Ltd v Secretary of State for Scotland* 1984 SLT 345 at 347 and E Young, 'Of public inquiry procedures, Delphic oracles and other things' (1983) 10 SPLP 75. See also *Ashbridge Investments Ltd v Minister of Housing and Local Government* [1965] 1 WLR 1320 and Rowan Robinson, *Scottish Planning Law and Procedure* (2001) paras 21.26A – 21.51.

question until the final determination of the proceedings; and

- if satisfied that the action in question is not within the powers of the 1997 Act, or that the interests of the applicant have been substantially prejudiced by failure to comply with any of the relevant requirements in relation to it, may quash the decision of the local review body.[23]

Where the decision of a local review body is quashed it will usually have the opportunity of reconsidering its actions in light of the court's opinion. The local review body may subsequently determine the application in a legally sustainable way and reach the same outcome. As noted above, it does not necessarily follow that, if the original decision is quashed, the decision will change when the application is reconsidered. However in some cases a change in circumstances (such as in planning policy) in the intervening period between the date of original decision and the date of the re-determination of the application for planning permission may mean that the decision (or the detail of the decision) changes.

Petition in an application to the Court of Session for judicial review

The Court of Session possesses at common law a supervisory jurisdiction which empowers it to ensure that all inferior courts, tribunals and other bodies possessing a limited jurisdiction act in accordance with the jurisdiction conferred upon them.[24] The grounds for judicial review fall under three broad headings:

- illegality;
- irrationality; and
- procedural impropriety

and these are considered in more detail below.

---

23 1997 Act, s 239(5).
24 On judicial review generally see Clyde & Edwards, *Judicial Review* (2000) and on judicial review in planning see The Hon Lord Reed 'Judicial Review', *Scottish Planning Encyclopedia*, vol 1, ch 11.

Where there is no statutory right available for review by the courts, the possibility arises of issuing a petition for judicial review of an act, decision or omission of a local review body.[25] Judicial review would be competent for instance where:

- an issue was raised about the compatibility of the local review process with the European Convention on Human Rights guaranteed under the Human Rights Act 1998;[26]
- a planning authority fails to act in accordance with the European Convention on Human Rights guaranteed under the Human Rights Act 1998, including its failure to determine an application within a reasonable time;[27]
- a planning authority refuses to accept an objection for consideration;[28] or
- a planning authority fails to conclude a planning obligation made under section 75 of the 1997 Act.[29]

Time limit for making an application for judicial review

Section 89 of the Courts Reform (Scotland) Act 2014 inserts new sections 27A–27D into the Court of Session Act 1988 and provides:

- as a general rule a time limit of three months beginning with the date on which the grounds giving rise to the application first arise for a petition for judicial review to be brought; and
- a new requirement to seek leave from the Court of Session before a petition for judicial review can proceed – this includes satisfying the court that the petitioner has 'sufficient interest' in the subject matter of the application for judicial review and that the application 'has a real prospect of success'.

---

25 Court of Session Rules, r 58.3.
26 See, eg, *County Properties Ltd v Scottish Ministers* 2001 SLT 1125.
27 See, eg, *Lafarge Redland Aggregates Ltd v Scottish Ministers* 2000 SLT 1361.
28 See, g, *Pollock v Secretary of State for Scotland* 1993 SLT 1173.
29 See, eg, *John G Russell (Transport) Ltd v Strathkelvin District Council*, 1992 SLT 1001.

Section 89 of the Courts Reform (Scotland) Act 2014 comes into force on 22 September 2015.

In the meantime there is no specific time limit within which judicial review proceedings must be brought and no judicial sifting of petitions for judicial review to identify those which are allowed to proceed. However, the longer the period before a petition for judicial review is presented the greater the risk of the petition being refused on the basis of 'mora, taciturnity and acquiescence'.[30]

Standing

In 2011 the Supreme Court in *Axa General Insurance Ltd v Lord Advocate*[31] signalled the time had come to move away from the restrictive test of an applicant's standing being based on both 'title to sue' and 'interest to sue'.

The test, the court said, should be based on interests rather than rights, since public authorities can violate the rule of law without infringing the rights of any individual. The court did not offer a precise definition but reaffirmed the need to exclude the 'mere busybody' and indicated that the words 'directly affected' were the essence of what is required. Lord Reed referred to 'sufficient interest' noting that what qualifies as sufficient interest will depend on the particular context.

Grounds for judicial review

As we noted above the grounds for judicial review fall under three broad headings. The grounds under those headings can be summarised as:

- *illegality*: the decision-maker must understand correctly the law that regulates the decision-making power and must give effect to it;

---

30 See, eg, *Bova and Christie v Highland Council* [2013] CSIH 41 and [2011] CSOH 140; *Portobello Park Action Group v City of Edinburgh Council* [2012] CSIH 69 and [2012] CSOH 38; and *Dulce Packard v Scottish Ministers* [2011] CSOH 93.

31 [2011] UKSC 46.

- *irrationality*: often referred to as '*Wednesbury* unreasonableness', ie the decision was so unreasonable that no reasonable authority could ever have come to it; and
- *procedural impropriety*: encompasses not only the failure to follow procedural rules set out in legislation but also any failure to observe the principles of natural justice or act with procedural fairness towards a person who will be affected by the decision (including the rule against bias (*nemo iudex in causa sua*), the right to a hearing (*audi alteram partem*) and the principle that justice must not only be done it must also be seen to be done).[32]

Court orders

The court, in exercising its supervisory jurisdiction on a petition for judicial review, may:

- grant or refuse any part of the petition, with or without conditions;
- make such order in relation to the act, decision or omission in question as it thinks fit, whether or not such order was sought in the petition, being an order that could be made if sought in any action or petition, including an order for reduction, declarator, suspension, interdict, implement, restitution, payment (whether of damages or otherwise) and any interim order; or
- subject to the relevant Court of Session Rules, make such order in relation to procedure as it thinks fit.[33]

As we noted above, if the court finds that the planning authority has acted unlawfully it will, in general, require the planning authority to reconsider its act or decision in a proper (lawful) manner.

---

32 See, eg, *R (on the application of Ashley) v Secretary of State for Communities and Local Government and Another* [2012] EWCA Civ 559; and *R (on the application of Tait) v Secretary of State for Communities and Local Government* [2012] EWHC 643 (Admin).
33 Court of Session Rules, r 58.4.

General comments about complaints

The decision of a local review body will stand unless it is set aside by a court;[34] its decision to grant planning permission is revoked or modified; or is the subject of a discontinuance order made by the planning authority.[35]

A successful complaint will not alter the decision of a local review body. However, a successful complaint might result in a remedy, such as the planning authority waiving the fee for a new planning permission application, which will benefit the persons making the complaint. Alternatively the outcome of a complaint might be that the planning authority will learn lessons and take steps to minimise the risk of a similar issue arising in the future.

A general overview about complaints is set out below. In some instances it is necessary to raise the complaint first with the person being complained about, for instance, the lawyer in the case of the Scottish Legal Complaints Commission, and the planning authority in the case of the Scottish Public Services Ombudsman, before proceeding to lodge a formal complaint, and there are detailed rules, for instance about the time limit for making a complaint.

Complaints to a local authority's Monitoring Officer

Any council constituted under section 2 of the Local Government etc (Scotland) Act 1994 has to designate one of its officers, other than the council's chief finance officer, as its 'Monitoring Officer'.[36] The Council's Head of Legal Services is usually a council's Monitoring Officer.

In general a Monitoring Officer has a duty to prepare a report where it appears that any proposal or decision of, or omission by the council, its committees, sub-committees or officers has given rise to, or is likely to or would give rise to:

- a contravention of any enactment or rule of law;
- a contravention of any code of practice made or approved under any enactment; or

---

34 See, eg, *The Firm of Archid v Dundee City Council* [2013] CSOH 137.
35 1997 Act, ss 65 and 71 respectively.
36 Local Government and Housing Act 1989, ss 5 and 5A.

- any maladministration or injustice.[37]

It would, for instance, be possible to raise a complaint with a council's Monitoring Officer regarding an officer wrongly insisting that a planning permission application can be determined by an officer under delegated powers.

While material is made available to a local review body, including an officer's report on handling, there is no further report to the local review body about the notice of review. Absent such a further report there is less of a focus on matters that might be raised with a council's Monitoring Officer than would normally be the case where officer reports are routinely submitted to other council committees.

However once the local review body gives its decision notice it appears that the appropriate avenue for complaint would, depending on the circumstances, be to the Court of Session (see above) or one of the bodies referred to below.

Complaints to the Commissioner for Ethical Standards in Public Life in Scotland and the Standards Commission for Scotland

The Standards Commission for Scotland, established under the Ethical Standards in Public Life etc (Scotland) Act 2000, is an independent public body which encourages high ethical standards in public life through the promotion and enforcement of Codes of Conduct for councillors and those appointed to the boards of devolved public bodies.

Councillors from all 32 councils must observe *The Councillors' Code of Conduct*.[38] The Cairngorms National Park Authority[39] and the Loch Lomond and The Trossachs National Park Authority[40]

---

37 As regards maladministration and injustice see *Scottish Public Services Ombudsman complaints* below.

38 www.gov.scot/Resource/Doc/334603/0109379.pdf

39 www.cairngorms.co.uk/park-authority/about-us/board

40 www.lochlomond-trossachs.org/looking-after/code-of-conduct/menu-id-420.html

are among the public bodies which have their own *Members' Code of Conduct*. Those codes include provisions about lobbying and access and taking decisions on planning matters. Further details are set out in Chapter 3.

The Commissioner for Ethical Standards in Public Life in Scotland ('the Commissioner') is an independent officeholder who considers complaints about a councillor or member of a devolved public body who is alleged to have contravened the *Councillors' Code of Conduct* or the appropriate *Members' Code of Conduct* of a public body.[41] The Commissioner was established from 1 July 2013, under the Public Services Reform (Commissioner for Ethical Standards in Public Life in Scotland etc) Order 2013,[42] to replace the Public Standards Commissioner for Scotland.

Where appropriate, the Commissioner will report on the outcome of these investigations to the Standards Commission for Scotland. The Standards Commission for Scotland may disqualify,[43] suspend[44] or censure[45] councillors or members.

Royal Town Planning Institute complaints

Members of the Royal Town Planning Institute ('RTPI') must observe the RTPI's *Code of Professional Conduct*.[46] That code states that RTPI members must in all their professional activities act with competence, honesty and integrity and includes other requirements such as that members:

- shall not make or subscribe to any statements or reports which are contrary to their own bona fide professional opinions; and

---

41 See www.ethicalstandards.org.uk

42 SSI 2013/197.

43 See, eg, (2010) 140 SPEL 85.

44 See, eg, (2012) 150 SPEL 37.

45 All Standards Commission decisions at www.standardscommissionscotland.org.uk/fulllist

46 www.rtpi.org.uk/media/8590/Code-of-Professional-Conduct-Final-_2_Jan-2012.pdf

- must take steps to ensure that their private, personal, political and financial interests do not conflict with their professional duties.

If the appointed officer, the local review body's planning adviser or a member of the local review body is a member of the RTPI and there is a failure to observe the RTPI's *Code of Professional Conduct*, a complaint may be made to the RTPI.[47]

Complaints to the Scottish Legal Complaints Commission

As we noted in Chapter 6, the Scottish Government has recognised the need for a local review body to have support from legal advisers. Further it is possible that a member of a local review body may be a solicitor, an advocate, a member of the Association of Commercial Attorneys or a conveyancing or executry practitioner (all hereinafter referred to as 'lawyer').

The Scottish Legal Complaints Commission ('SLCC') was established under the Legal Profession and Legal Aid (Scotland) Act 2007. If a complaint has been made against a lawyer and the lawyer has been unable to resolve it, the complaint should be addressed to the SLCC.

The SLCC will review the complaints that it receives. Any complaint about the conduct of a lawyer, including complaints about their behaviour or fitness to carry out work, will be passed to the relevant professional organisation such as the Law Society of Scotland or the Faculty of Advocates. Any complaint about the service provided by a lawyer including complaints about the quality of work a practitioner has carried out will be considered by the SLCC.[48]

---

47 See www.rtpi.org.uk/membership/professional-standards/how-to-make-a-complaint-about-rtpi-members
48 See www.scottishlegalcomplaints.com

Scottish Public Services Ombudsman complaints

The Scottish Public Services Ombudsman ('SPSO') was established by the Scottish Public Services Ombudsman Act 2002. The SPSO looks into the complaints of a person who claims to have suffered injustice or hardship as a result of maladministration or service failure by public bodies including councils and the two national park authorities. The SPSO, like the SLCC, is an option of last resort. It will only look at complaints which have not been resolved once the formal complaints procedure of the organisation concerned has been exhausted.

The Scottish Public Services Ombudsman Act 2002 does not define 'injustice' or 'hardship'. However those terms can include: hurt feelings, distress, worry, or inconvenience; loss of right or amenity; financial loss or unnecessary expense, time and trouble in pursuing a justified complaint. There has to be some evidence of maladministration or service failure.

The Scottish Public Services Ombudsman Act 2002 does not define 'maladministration'. The 'Crossman catalogue' gives 'bias, neglect, inattention, delay, incompetence, ineptitude, perversity, turpitude and arbitrariness and so on' as examples of maladministration.

Maladministration can be grouped under headings such as 'administrative shortcomings' (such as giving misleading advice); 'bad conduct' (for instance discourtesy) and 'faulty exercise of discretion' (for example inconsistency in decisions).[49] The term 'service failure' encompasses failure in a service provided or failure to provide a service that should be provided.

The SPSO provides general advice about how to complain[50] and has published leaflets about the type of complaints that may be made by those involved (including applicants and objectors) in planning matters including what the SPSO can, and cannot, look into.[51]

---

49 J Logie and P Watchman *The Local Ombudsman* (1990).

50 See www.spso.org.uk/how-complain

51 See www.spso.org.uk/information-leaflets

Town and Country Planning (Scotland) Act 1997

43A   Local developments: schemes of delegation

(1) A planning authority are—

(a) as soon as practicable after the coming into force of section 17 of the Planning etc (Scotland) Act 2006 (asp 17), and thereafter—

  (i) whenever required to do so by the Scottish Ministers, or

  (ii) subject to sub-paragraph (i), at such intervals as may be provided for in regulations under this section,

to prepare a scheme (to be known as a 'scheme of delegation') by which any application for planning permission for a development within the category of local developments or any application for consent, agreement or approval required by a condition imposed on a grant of planning permission for a development within that category is to be determined by a person appointed by them for the purposes of this section instead of by them, and

(b) to keep under review the scheme so prepared.

(2) Other than for the purposes of subsections (8) to (16) or section 47, the determination of any person so appointed is to be treated as that of the authority.

(3) References in subsection (1) to a development do not include references to a development of a class mentioned in section 38A(1).

(4) Without prejudice to subsection (1)(a)(ii), regulations under this section may make provision as to—

(a) the form and content of, and

(b) the procedures for preparing and adopting,

a scheme of delegation.

(5) Where an application for planning permission falls to be determined by a person so appointed, sections 27A(2), 27B(2), 30(3), 32A(3), 37(1) to (3), 38, 39, 40, 41(1) and (2), 42, 43(1) to (2), 46, 58, 59 and 60(5) and Part 1 of Schedule 3 apply, with any necessary modifications (including, in the case of that Part, the modification mentioned in subsection (18)), as they apply to an application which falls to be determined by the planning authority.

(6) The planning authority may, if they think fit, decide themselves to determine an application which would otherwise fall to be determined by a person so appointed.

(7) Any such decision must include a statement of the reasons for which it has been taken; and a copy of the decision is to be served on the applicant.

(8) Where a person so appointed—

(a) refuses an application for planning permission or for consent, agreement or approval,

(b) grants it subject to conditions, or

(c) has not determined it within such period as may be prescribed by regulations or a development order, or within such extended period as may at any time be agreed upon in writing between the applicant and the person so appointed

the applicant may require the planning authority to review the case.

(8A) A requirement to review may not be made by virtue of paragraph (c) of subsection (8) if within the period (or extended period) mentioned in that paragraph notice has been given to the applicant that—

(a) the power under section 39 to decline to determine the application has been exercised; or

(b) the application has been referred to the Scottish Ministers in accordance with directions given under section 46.

(9) Where a requirement to review is made by virtue of paragraph (c) of subsection (8), the person so appointed is, for the purposes of the review, to be deemed to have decided to refuse the application.

(10) Regulations or a development order may make provision as to the form and procedures of any review conducted by virtue of subsection (8).

(11) Without prejudice to the generality of subsection (10), the regulations or order may—

(a) make different provision for different cases or classes of case,

(b) make different provision for different stages of a case,

(c) make provision in relation to oral or written submissions and to documents in support of such submissions,

(d) make provision in relation to time limits (including a time limit for requiring the review), and

(e) require the planning authority to give to the person who has required the review such notice as may be prescribed by the regulations or the order as to the manner in which that review has been dealt with.

(12) Any notice given by virtue of paragraph (e) of subsection (11)—

(a) is to include a statement of—

(i) the terms in which the planning authority have decided the case reviewed, and

(ii) the reasons on which the authority based that decision, and

(b) may include such other information as may be prescribed by the regulations or the order.

(13) The provision which may be made by virtue of subsections (10) and (11) includes provision as to—

(a) the making of oral submissions, or as to any failure to make such submissions or to lodge documents in support of such submissions, or

(b) the lodging of, or as to any failure to lodge, written submissions or documents in support of such submissions,

and, subject to section 43B, as to what matters may be raised in the course of the review.

(14) The provision which may be made by virtue of subsections (10) and (11) includes provision that the manner in which the review, or any stage of the review, is to be conducted (as for example whether oral submissions are to be made or written submissions lodged) is to be at the discretion of the planning authority.

(15) The planning authority may uphold, reverse or vary a determination reviewed by them by virtue of subsection (8).

(16) Subject to subsection (17) and except as provided under section 239, the decision of a planning authority in a case reviewed under this section is final.

(17) Where a requirement to review is made by virtue of para-

graph (c) of subsection (8) and the planning authority have not conducted the review within such period as may be prescribed by regulations or a development order, the authority are to be deemed to have decided to refuse the application and section 47(1) is to apply accordingly.

(18) The modification is that, in paragraph 1(6) of Schedule 3, for paragraph (b) there is substituted—

'(b) is to be regarded for the purposes of section 43A as a condition imposed by a decision of the appointed person, and may accordingly be the subject of a review under subsection (8) of that section.'.

43B   Matters which may be raised in a review under section 43A(8)

(1) In a review under section 43A(8), a party to the proceedings is not to raise any matter which was not before the appointed person at the time the determination reviewed was made unless that party can demonstrate—

(a) that the matter could not have been raised before that time, or

(b) that its not being raised before that time was a consequence of exceptional circumstances.

(2) Nothing in subsection (1) affects any requirement or entitlement to have regard to—

(a) the provisions of the development plan, or

(b) any other material consideration.

237   Validity of development plans and certain orders, decisions and directions.

(1) Except as provided by this Part, the validity of—

. . .

(f) any such action on the part of the Secretary of State as is mentioned in subsection (3), or on the part of a planning authority as is mentioned in subsection (3A)

shall not be questioned in any legal proceedings whatsoever.

. . .

(3A) The action on the part of a planning authority is any decision or determination (other than a deemed decision) in a review conducted by them by virtue of section 43A(8).

(4) Nothing in this section shall affect the exercise of any juris-

diction of any court in respect of any refusal or failure on the part of the Secretary of State to take any such action as is mentioned in subsection (3) or on the part of a planning authority to take any such action as is mentioned in subsection (3A).

239 Proceedings for questioning the validity of other orders, decisions and directions.

(1) If any person—

(a) is aggrieved by any order to which this section applies and wishes to question the validity of that order on the grounds—

    (i) that the order is not within the powers of this Act, or

    (ii) that any of the relevant requirements have not been complied with in relation to that order, or

(b) is aggrieved by any action on the part of the Secretary of State, or on the part of a planning authority, to which this section applies and wishes to question the validity of that action on the grounds—

    (i) that the action is not within the powers of this Act, or

    (ii) that any of the relevant requirements have not been complied with in relation to that action,

he may make an application to the Court of Session under this section.

. . .

(3) An application under this section must be made within 6 weeks from the date on which the order is confirmed (or, in the case of an order under section 65 which takes effect under section 67 without confirmation, the date on which it takes effect) or, as the case may be, the date on which the action is taken.

(4) This section applies to any such order as is mentioned in sub-section (2) of section 237 and to any such action on the part of the Secretary of State as is mentioned in subsection (3) of that section or on the part of a planning authority as is mentioned in subsection (3A) of that section.

Appendix II

Town and Country Planning (Schemes of Delegation and Local Review Procedure) (Scotland) Regulations 2013 (SSI 2013/157)

PART 1
PRELIMINARY

1 Citation, commencement and application

(1) These Regulations may be cited as the Town and Country Planning (Schemes of Delegation and Local Review Procedure) (Scotland) Regulations 2013 and come into force on 30th June 2013.

(2) These Regulations (other than Part 2) apply to reviews conducted by virtue of section 43A(8) of the Act.

(3) Part 2 of these Regulations applies to the preparation and content of a scheme of delegation under section 43A(1) of the Act.

2 Interpretation

In these Regulations—

'Act' means the Town and Country Planning (Scotland) Act 1997;

'appointed officer' means a person appointed by virtue of a scheme of delegation under section 43A(1) of the Act by the planning authority to determine the application;

'EIA development' has the same meaning as in the Town and Country Planning (Environmental Impact Assessment) (Scotland) Regulations 2011;

'hearing session' means a hearing held or to be held into matters specified in a procedure notice given under rule 1(1) of the Hearing Session Rules;

'Hearing Session Rules' means the rules set out in Schedule 1 to these Regulations;

'interested party' means—

(a) any authority or person consulted by the planning authority in compliance with a requirement imposed by virtue of section 43(1)(c) of the Act and from whom the planning authority received representations (which were not subsequently withdrawn) in connection with the application; and

(b) any other person from whom the planning authority received representations (which were not subsequently withdrawn) in connection with the application, before the end of the period mentioned in section 38(1) of the Act;

'local review body' has the meaning given in regulation 7(1);

'period allowed for determination of the application' means the period prescribed under regulation 8(2) in respect of the application or such extended period as may be agreed in writing between the applicant and the appointed officer under section 43A(8)(c);

'procedure notice' means a notice given (whether separately or in combination) under regulation 15(1) or rule 1(1) of the Hearing Session Rules;

'reference number of the application' means the unique number assigned by the planning authority to the application;

'review documents' means notice of the decision in respect of the application to which the review relates, the Report on Handling and any documents referred to in that Report, the notice of review given in accordance with regulation 9, all documents accompanying the notice of review in accordance with regulation 9(4) and any representations or comments made under regulation 10(4) or (6) in relation to the review;

'Report on Handling' means, in respect of an application, the report to be placed in the register of applications which the planning authority are required to keep in accordance with regulations made under section 36(1) of the Act;

'rule' means a rule set out in Schedule 1 to these Regulations; and

'specified matters' are in relation to a request for further written representations or information under regulation 15 or to a particular hearing session, those matters which are set out in the procedure notice; and

'validation date' has—

(a) in the case of an application for planning permission for EIA development, the same meaning as in regulation 44(2)(b) of the Town and Country Planning (Environmental Impact Assessment) (Scotland) Regulations 2011; and

(b) in any other case, the same meaning as in the Town and Country Planning (Development Management Procedure) (Scotland) Regulations 2013.

PART 2
SCHEMES OF DELEGATION

3   Content of scheme of delegation

(1) A scheme of delegation must describe the classes of development to which the scheme will apply and state with respect to every such class which of the applications mentioned in paragraph (2) are to be determined by an appointed officer and if such application is only to be so determined in particular circumstances the scheme is to specify such circumstances.

(2) The applications are—

(a) applications for planning permission; and

(b) applications for consent, agreement or approval required by a condition imposed on a grant of planning permission.

4   Procedure for preparation and adoption of scheme of delegation

Where a planning authority propose to adopt a scheme of delegation, the authority must send a copy of the scheme to the Scottish Ministers and the planning authority must not adopt the scheme until the scheme has been approved by the Scottish Ministers.

5   Publication of the scheme

The planning authority must—

(a) make a copy of the adopted scheme of delegation available for inspection at an office of the planning authority and in every public library in the area of the planning authority; and

(b) publish the adopted scheme of delegation on the internet.

6   Subsequent schemes of delegation

The planning authority must prepare a scheme of delegation at intervals of no greater than every five years.

PART 3
REVIEW

7 Local Review Body

(1) A review of a case by virtue of section 43A(8) of the Act is to be conducted by a committee of the planning authority comprising at least three members of the authority (to be known as the 'local review body').

(2) Meetings of the local review body at which decisions—

(a) under regulation 13 relating to the manner in which the review is to be conducted; or

(b) as to how the case under review is to be determined,

are to be held in public.

(3) The date, time and place at which a meeting mentioned in paragraph (2) is to be held is to be determined (and may subsequently be varied) by the local review body.

(4) The local review body must give to—

(a) the applicant; and

(b) any interested parties who made representations (which were not subsequently withdrawn) in connection with the application under regulation 10(4),

such notice of the date, time and place fixed for the holding of such meeting (and any subsequent variation thereof) as may appear to the local review body to be reasonable in the circumstances.

8 Review on failure to determine the application

(1) An applicant may require the local review body to review the case under section 43A(8)(c) of the Act if the appointed officer has failed to give to the applicant notice of their decision or determination within the period allowed for determination of the application.

(2) The period prescribed for the purposes of section 43A(8)(c) of the Act is—

(a) in the case of an application for planning permission for EIA development, the period of four months after the validation date; and

(b) in any other case, the period of two months after the validation date.

(3) The period prescribed for the purposes of section 43A(17) of the Act is the period of three months beginning on the date

when the requirement to review is made by virtue of section 43A(8)(c) of the Act.

9   Notice of Review

(1) An applicant may require the local review body to review a case under section 43A(8) by giving notice in writing in accordance with this regulation.

(2) The notice of review must be served on the local review body within the period of three months beginning with, in the case of a requirement arising by virtue of—

(a) section 43A(8)(a) or (b) of the Act, the date of the notice of the decision to which the review relates;

(b) section 43(8)(c) of the Act, the date of expiry of the period allowed for determination of the application.

(3) The notice of review (on a form obtained from the planning authority) must include—

(a) the name and address of the applicant;

(b) the date and the reference number of the application in respect of which the review is required;

(c) the name and address of the representative of the applicant (if any) and whether any notice or other correspondence which is required by these Regulations to be sent to the applicant should be sent to the representative instead of the applicant; and

(d) a statement setting out the applicant's reasons for requiring the local review body to review the case and by what, if any, procedure (or combination of procedures) mentioned in regulation 13(4) the applicant considers the review should be conducted.

(4) Subject to paragraph (5)—

(a) all matters which the applicant intends to raise in the review must be set out in the notice of review or in the documents which accompany the notice of review; and

(b) all documents, materials and evidence which the applicant intends to rely on in the review must accompany the notice of review.

(5) In addition to matters set out in the notice of review and documents which accompany the notice of review, the applicant may raise matters and submit further documents, materials or evidence only in accordance with and to the extent permitted by regulation 15 and the Hearing Session Rules.

10   Notification to interested parties and publication

(1) The local review body must not later than 14 days following notification of the review—

(a) send an acknowledgement of the notice of review to the applicant and inform the applicant how documents related to the review may be inspected; and

(b) give notice of the review to each interested party.

(2) Notice under paragraph (1)(b) may be given—

(a) by post to any interested party notified or consulted under the Act other than by newspaper advertisement; and

(b) by post or by advertisement in a newspaper circulating in the locality where the proposed development is situated, to any other interested party.

(3) Notice under paragraph (1)(b) is to—

(a) state the name of the applicant and the address of the site to which the review relates;

(b) describe the application;

(c) state that copies of any representations previously made with respect to the application, will be considered by the local review body when determining the review;

(d) state that further representations may be made to the local review body and include information as to how any representations may be made, by what date they must be made and that a copy of the representation will be sent to the applicant for comment; and

(e) state how a copy of the notice of review and other documents related to the review may be inspected.

(4) An interested party may, within 14 days beginning with the date on which notice is given under paragraph (1)(b) make representations in respect of the review to the local review body.

(5) The local review body must send a copy of any representations received under paragraph (4) to the applicant and must inform the applicant how and by what date (being a date not less than 14 days after the date on which such copy is sent under this paragraph) the applicant may make comments to the local review body on such representations.

(6) The applicant may, on or before that date, make comments on such representations to the local review body.

11   Publication of review documents

(1) The planning authority must, in relation to a review, make a copy of—

(a) the review documents;

(b) any notice given under regulation 10(1); and

(c) any procedure notice,

available for inspection at an office of the planning authority until such time as the review is determined.

(2) The planning authority are until such time as the review is determined to afford to any person who so requests the opportunity to inspect and, where practicable, take copies of any review documents (or any part thereof).

PART 4
PROCEDURE FOR DETERMINATION

12   Determination without further procedure

Where the local review body consider that the review documents provide sufficient information to enable them to determine the review, they may determine the review without further procedure.

13   Decision as to procedure to be followed

(1) Where the local review body do not determine the review without further procedure, the local review body may determine the manner in which the review is to be conducted and are to do so in accordance with this regulation.

(2) The local review body may determine at any stage of the review that further representations should be made or further information should be provided to enable them to determine the review.

(3) Where the local review body so determine, the review or a stage of the review is to be conducted by one of, or by a combination of, the procedures mentioned in paragraph (4).

(4) The procedures are—

(a) by means of written submissions;

(b) by the holding of one or more hearing sessions; and

(c) by means of an inspection of the land to which the review relates.

(5) Where the local review body consider that such further representations should be made or information should be made available or provided by means of—

(a) written submissions, regulation 15 applies;

(b) a hearing session, the Hearing Session Rules apply; or

(c) an inspection of the land, regulation 16 applies.

(6) Notices given under regulation 15(1) or rule 1(1) of the Hearing Session Rules may be given separately or combined into a single notice.

14 Pre-examination meetings

(1) The local review body may hold a meeting ('a pre-examination meeting') to consider the manner in which the review or any stage of the review is to be conducted with a view to securing that the review or any stage of the review is conducted efficiently and expeditiously.

(2) The local review body are to determine (and may subsequently vary) the date, time and place for the holding of a pre-examination meeting.

(3) The local review body must give such notice of the holding of a pre-examination meeting and of the date, time and place where it is to be held (and any subsequent variation thereof) as may appear to the local review body to be reasonable in the circumstances—

(a) where a pre-examination meeting is to be held in connection only with the conduct of a particular hearing session, to those persons entitled to appear at that hearing session; and

(b) in any other case to the applicant, to the planning authority and any interested party.

(4) The local review body are to determine the matters to be discussed and the procedure to be followed at the pre-examination meeting.

(5) In this regulation 'pre-examination meeting' has the meaning given in paragraph (1).

15 Written submissions

(1) Where the local review body has determined that further representations should be made or further information should be provided by means of written submissions, the local review body may request such further representations or information and is to do so by giving written notice to that effect to—

(a) the applicant; and

(b) any other body or person from whom the local review body wishes to receive further representations or information.

(2) The procedure notice given under paragraph (1) is to—

(a) set out the matters on which such further representations or information is requested;

(b) specify the date by which such further representations or information are to be sent to the appointed person; and

(c) provide the name and address of any body or person to whom the procedure notice is given.

(3) Any further representations made or information provided in response to the procedure notice ('the procedure notice response') are to be sent to the local review body on or before the date specified for that purpose in the procedure notice and a copy of any procedure notice response is to be sent on or before that date to any other person or body to whom the procedure notice was given.

(4) Within a period of 14 days from receipt of a copy of the procedure notice response, any body or person to whom the procedure notice was given—

(a) may send comments to the local review body in reply to the procedure notice response; and

(b) must when doing so send a copy of such comments to any other person or body to whom the procedure notice was given.

(5) A copy of any procedure notice response or any comments required to be sent to a body or person under this regulation is to be sent to the body or person at the address provided for the body or person in the procedure notice.

(6) In this regulation 'procedure notice response' has the meaning given in paragraph (3).

16   Site inspections

(1) The local review body may at any time make—

(a) an unaccompanied inspection of the land to which the review relates; or

(b) an inspection of the land in the company of such of the persons notified under paragraph (3) as desire to attend the inspection.

(2) Where the local review body intend to make an unaccompanied inspection, the local review body are to inform the applicant that they propose to do so.

(3) Where the local review body intend to make an accompanied inspection, the local review body are to give such notice of the date and time of the proposed inspection as may appear to them to be reasonable in the circumstances to—

(a) the applicant; and

(b) any interested party.

(4) The local review body is not bound to defer an inspection if any person to whom notice was given under paragraph (3) is not present at the time appointed.

17 New evidence

(1) If, after the conclusion of any further procedure conducted by virtue of regulation 13, the local review body propose to take into consideration any new evidence which is material to the determination of the review, the local review body must not reach a decision on the review without first affording the applicant and any other relevant party an opportunity of making representations on such new evidence.

(2) In this regulation 'relevant party' means—

  (i) where the new evidence relates to a specified matter considered at a hearing session, any person entitled to appear at that hearing session;

  (ii) where the new evidence relates to matters in respect of which further written representations or information was sought by a procedure notice under regulation 15, any person to whom such notice was sent.

PART 5

GENERAL

18 National security

The validity of a notice of review is not affected by failure to disclose information as to—

(a) national security; and

(b) the measures taken, or to be taken, to ensure the security of any premises or property,

where the notice of review is accompanied by a written statement from the applicant that, in the opinion of the applicant, the information relates to the matters mentioned in paragraph (a) or (b) above, and that public disclosure of that information would be contrary to the national interest.

19   Further copies of documents etc

(1) The local review body may require any person who has submitted documents, materials or evidence under these Regulations in connection with the review to—

(a) provide to the local review body such number of additional copies of such of those documents, materials or evidence as they may specify; and

(b) provide to such other persons as they may specify such copies or additional copies of any documents, materials or evidence as they may specify.

(2) The planning authority must, until such time as the review is determined, make copies of such documents, materials or evidence provided under paragraph (1)(a) available for inspection at an office of the planning authority and, where practicable, must afford any person who so requests a reasonable opportunity of taking copies of such documents (or any part thereof).

20   Compliance with development management procedures

The local review body must, to the extent not already done so, comply with regulations 18 (notification by the planning authority), 19 (notification of minerals applications), 20 (publication of application by the planning authority) and 25 (consultation by the planning authority) of the Town and Country Planning (Development Management Procedure) (Scotland) Regulations 2013 before determining the review.

21   Appointment of assessor

(1) The local review body may appoint a person to sit with the local review body at a hearing session to advise them on such matters arising as they may specify ('an assessor') and where they do so they are to notify every person entitled to appear at the hearing session of the name of the assessor and of the matters on which the assessor is to advise them.

(2) Where an assessor has been appointed, the assessor may (and if so required by the local review body, must), after the close of the hearing session, make a report in writing to the local review body in respect of the matters on which the assessor was appointed to advise.

22   Decision Notice

(1) The local review body must—

(a) give notice ('a decision notice') of their decision to the applicant; and

(b) notify every person who has made (and not subsequently withdrawn) representations in respect of the review that a decision on the review has been made and where a copy of the decision notice is available for inspection.

(2) A decision notice must, in addition to the matters required by section 43A(12)(a) of the Act—

(a) in the case of an application for planning permission—

(i) include the reference number of the application;

(ii) include a description of the location of the proposed development including, where applicable, a postal address;

(iii) include a description of the proposed development (including identification of the plans and drawings showing the proposed development) for which planning permission has been granted, or as the case may be, refused;

(iv) include a description of any variation made to the application in accordance with section 32A of the Act;

(v) specify any conditions to which the decision is subject;

(vi) include a statement as to the effect of section 58(2) or 59(4) of the Act, as the case may be, or where the planning authority have made a direction under section 58(2) or 59(5) of the Act, give details of that direction;

(vii) if any obligation is to be entered into under section 75 of the Act in connection with the application, state where the terms of such obligation or a summary of such terms may be inspected; and

(viii) include details of the provisions of the development plan and any other material considerations to which the local review body had regard in determining the application;

(b) in the case of an application for a consent, agreement or approval required by a condition imposed on a grant of planning permission include—

(i) a description of the matter in respect of which approval,

consent or agreement has been granted or, as the case
may be, refused;

(ii) the reference number of the application; and

(iii) the reference number of the application for the planning
permission in respect of which the condition in question
was imposed.

(3) A decision notice must in the case of refusal or approval subject to conditions be accompanied by a notification in the terms
set out in Schedule 2 to these Regulations.

23   Electronic communications

(1) Where the criteria in paragraph (2) are met, any document required or authorised to be sent by these Regulations
may be sent by electronic communications and any requirement
in these Regulations that any document is to be in writing is
fulfilled.

(2) The criteria are—

(a) the recipient consents, or is deemed to have agreed under
paragraph (3), to receive it electronically; and

(b) that the document transmitted by the electronic communication is—

(i) capable of being accessed by the recipient;

(ii) legible in all material respects; and

(iii) sufficiently permanent to be used for subsequent reference.

(3) The local review body and any person sending a document
using electronic communications are to be taken to have agreed—

(a) to the use of such communications for all purposes relating
to the review which are capable of being carried out
electronically; and

(b) that the address for the purpose of such communications is
the address incorporated into, or otherwise logically associated with, that communication.

(4) Deemed agreement under paragraph (3) shall subsist until
that person gives notice to revoke the agreement.

(5) Notice of withdrawal of consent to the use of electronic
communications or of revocation of agreement under paragraph
(4) takes effect on a date specified by the person in the notice, but
not less than seven days after the date on which the notice is
given.

(6) In this regulation—

'address' includes any number or address used for the purpose of such communications or storage;

'document' includes any notice, consent, agreement, decision, representation, statement, report or other information or communication;

'electronic communication' has the meaning given in section 15(1) of the Electronic Communications Act 2000;

'legible in all material respects' means that the information contained in the document is available to the recipient to no lesser extent than it would be if sent or given by means of a document in printed form; and

'sent' includes served, submitted or given and cognate expressions are to be construed accordingly.

24   Revocations, saving and transitional provisions

(1) Subject to paragraph (3), the provisions specified in paragraph (2) are revoked.

(2) The provisions are—

(a) the 2008 Regulations;

(b) regulation 5 of the Town and Country Planning (Miscellaneous Amendments) (Scotland) Regulations 2009; and

(c) regulation 4 of the Town and Country Planning (Miscellaneous Amendments) (Scotland) Regulations 2011.

(3) In relation to a hearing session or inquiry session in respect of which notice is given under paragraph 1(1) of Schedule 1 (hearing session rules) of the 2008 Regulations before 30th June 2013—

(a) Schedule 1 (hearing session rules) of the 2008 Regulations continues to have effect as it did immediately before that date; and

(b) the Hearing Session Rules contained in these Regulations do not apply.

(4) In this regulation 'the 2008 Regulations' means the Town and Country Planning (Schemes of Delegation and Local Review Procedure) (Scotland) Regulations 2008.

SCHEDULE 1   Regulation 2
HEARING SESSION RULES

1   Procedure notice and specified matters

(1) Where the local review body have determined that a hearing session should be held the local review body are to give written notice to that effect to—

(a) the applicant;

(b) any interested party who made representations in relation to specified matters; and

(c) any other body or person from whom the local review body wish to receive further representations or to provide further information on specified matters at a hearing session.

(2) The notice given under paragraph (1) is to specify the matters which are to be considered at the hearing session.

(3) Only specified matters are to be considered at the hearing session.

(4) A person or body given notice under paragraph (1) and who intends to appear at the hearing session must within 14 days of the date of such notice inform the local review body in writing of that intention.

2   Appearances at hearing session

The persons entitled to appear at a hearing session are—

(a) the applicant; and

(b) any other person or body who, in response to a procedure notice, has informed the local review body of their intention to appear at the hearing session in accordance with rule 1(4).

3   Date and notification of hearing session

(1) The date, time and place at which the hearing session is to be held is to be determined (and may subsequently be varied) by the local review body.

(2) The local review body are to give to those persons entitled to appear at the hearing session such notice of the date, time and place fixed for the holding of a hearing session (and any subsequent variation thereof) as may appear to the local review body to be reasonable in the circumstances.

4   Service of hearing statements and documents

(1) A person entitled to appear at the hearing session must, by

such date as the local review body may by notice specify, send to the local review body, the applicant and to such other persons entitled to appear at the hearing session as the local review body may specify in such notice—

(a) a hearing statement; and

(b) where that person intends to refer to or rely on any documents when presenting their case—

  (i) a list of all such documents; and

  (ii) a copy of every document (or the relevant part of a document) on that list which is not already available for inspection under regulation 11 or 19(2) or paragraph (2) of this rule.

(2) The planning authority, until such time as the review is determined, are to afford to any person who so requests a reasonable opportunity to inspect and, where practicable, take copies of any hearing statement or other document (or any part thereof) which, or a copy of which, has been sent to the local review body in accordance with this rule.

(3) Any person who has served a hearing statement in accordance with this rule must—

(a) when required by notice in writing from the local review body provide such further information about the matters contained in the statement as the local review body may specify; and

(b) at the same time send a copy of such further information to any other person on whom the hearing statement has been served.

(4) Different dates and different persons may be specified for the purposes of paragraphs (1)(a) and (b).

(5) In this rule, 'hearing statement' means, and is comprised of—

(a) a written statement which fully sets out the case relating to the specified matters which a person proposes to put forward at a hearing session;

(b) a list of documents (if any) which the person putting forward such case intends to refer to or rely on; and

(c) a list of any other persons who are to speak at the hearing session in respect of such case, any matters which such persons are particularly to address and any relevant qualifications of such persons to do so.

5   Procedure at hearing

(1) Except as otherwise provided in these Hearing Session Rules, the local review body shall determine the procedure at a hearing session.

(2) The local review body, having considered any submission by the persons entitled to appear at the hearing session, are to state at or before the commencement of the hearing session the procedure which the local review body propose to adopt and in particular are to state—

  (a) the order in which the specified matters are to be considered at the hearing session; and

  (b) the order in which the persons entitled to appear at the hearing session are to be heard in relation to a specified matter (a different order may be chosen for different specific matters).

(3) Any person entitled to appear may do so on that person's own behalf or be represented by another person.

(4) Where there are two or more persons having a similar interest in the issues being considered at the hearing session, the local review body may allow one or more persons to appear on behalf of some or all of any persons so interested.

(5) A hearing shall take the form of a discussion led by the local review body and cross-examination is not permitted unless the local review body consider that cross-examination is required to ensure a thorough examination of the issues.

(6) Subject to paragraph (7) a person entitled to appear at a hearing session is entitled to call evidence.

(7) The local review body may refuse to permit—

  (a) the giving or production of evidence;

  (b) the cross-examination of persons giving evidence; or

  (c) the presentation of any other matter,

which the local review body consider to be irrelevant or repetitious.

(8) The local review body may proceed with a hearing session in the absence of any person entitled to appear at the hearing session.

(9) The local review body may from time to time adjourn the hearing session and are to give such notice of the date, time and place of the adjourned hearing session to the persons entitled to appear at the hearing session as may appear to them to be reasonable in the circumstances unless such date, time and place are announced before the adjournment, no further notice is required.

SCHEDULE 2   Regulation 22
NOTICE TO ACCOMPANY REFUSAL ETC

TOWN AND COUNTRY PLANNING (SCOTLAND) ACT 1997

Notification to be sent to applicant on refusal of planning permission or on the grant of permission subject to conditions

NOTICE TO ACCOMPANY REFUSAL ETC
TOWN AND COUNTRY PLANNING (SCOTLAND) ACT 1997

Notification to be sent to applicant on determination by the planning authority of an application following a review conducted under section 43A(8)

1 If the applicant is aggrieved by the decision of the planning authority—
   (a) to refuse permission for the proposed development;
   (b) to refuse approval, consent or agreement required by a condition imposed on a grant of planning permission; or
   (c) to grant permission or approval, consent or agreement subject to conditions,
the applicant may question the validity of that decision by making an application to the Court of Session. An application to the Court of Session must be made within 6 weeks of the date of the decision.

2 If permission to develop land is refused or granted subject to conditions and the owner of the land claims that the land has become incapable of reasonably beneficial use in its existing state and cannot be rendered capable of reasonably beneficial use by the carrying out of any development which has been or would be permitted, the owner of the land may serve on the planning authority a purchase notice requiring the purchase of the owner of the land's interest in the land in accordance with Part V of the Town and Country Planning (Scotland) Act 1997.

Appendix III

Circular 5/2013 Schemes of Delegation and Local Reviews

Introduction

1.   The planning system should operate in support of the Government's central purpose of creating a more successful country, with opportunities for all of Scotland to flourish, through increasing sustainable economic growth. For decision making this means providing greater certainty of process, including being timely and transparent, as a means to achieve better places for Scotland. Planning authorities use powers of delegation so that certain decisions can be taken by officials instead of being considered by elected members of the authority at committee. Delegation to officials is an important means of adding efficiency to administrative processes and the Scottish Government wants to encourage an appropriate level of delegation to officials to support the role of the planning system in achieving their central purpose.

Schemes of delegation and local reviews for local development

2.   This circular relates to the Town and Country Planning (Schemes of Delegation and Local Review Procedure) (Scotland) Regulations 2013[1] (the Regulations). It replaces Circular 7/2009 on Schemes of Delegation and Local Reviews, which is cancelled. It explains the requirements for preparing schemes of delegation and conducting local reviews contained in the Regulations and the Town and Country Planning (Scotland) Act 1997,[2] as amended (the 1997 Act). Unless otherwise stated, references to a particular

1 http://www.legislation.gov.uk/ssi/2013/157/contents/made
2 http://www.legislation.gov.uk/ukpga/1997/8/contents

regulation or to a section will be to the Regulations or the 1997 Act respectively. References to planning permission include planning permission in principle.

3.   These schemes of delegation relate to applications for planning permission for local development and applications for approval, consent or agreement required by a condition imposed on a grant of planning permission for a local development. Local developments are those which are not categorised as either major developments in the Town and Country Planning (Hierarchy of Developments) (Scotland) Regulations 2009[3] or as national developments in the National Planning Framework.

4.   Where a scheme of delegation under section 43A(1) of the 1997 Act delegates such applications to a person appointed to make a decision (usually an officer of the authority and hereafter referred to as an appointed officer), the applicant does not have a right of appeal to Scottish Ministers against either the decision or the failure of the appointed officer to take a decision within the period for determination.[4] Instead the applicant has a right to a review by the planning authority of the decision or the failure to determine the application.

5.   Where the applications mentioned in paragraph 3 are not determined by an appointed officer, the applicant has a right of appeal to Scottish Ministers. This may be the case because the terms of the scheme trigger referral of the application to members for a decision, or where the planning authority exercise the power to take specific applications out of the scheme of delegation (see paragraph 18).

Changes to legislation

6.   The Regulations incorporate the minor amendments previously made to the Town and Country Planning (Schemes of Delegation and Local Review Procedures) (Scotland) Regulations

---

3   http://www.legislation.gov.uk/ssi/2009/51/contents/made

4   Two months (four months where environmental impact assessment is required) from the validation date or any extended period agreed upon in writing by the applicant and the planning authority.

2008 (which are now revoked), and make other minor amendments to improve consistency and clarity. However, the main
changes made by the Regulations are:

- the removal of the requirement for schemes of delegation to
  include a restriction on delegating planning authority interest
  cases;
- the extension from two to three months of the period within
  which a local review body must deal with a review sought
  on the grounds of non-determination, before the deemed
  refusal of permission applies; and
- a 'hearing statement' must now 'fully set out' the case, (rather
  than the previous requirement to 'outline' the case).

7.   Information on the transitional arrangements for these changes
(previously available online) is at paragraphs 60 to 62.

8.   The provisions are intended to promote efficient and high
quality decision making. The Scottish Government's intention is
that planning authorities should make the most effective use of
powers to delegate decisions on straightforward planning applications to officials, allowing elected members to focus attention on
more complex or controversial applications. The approach taken
in the Regulations is to provide planning authorities with significant scope to develop schemes of delegation that are appropriate to
local circumstances and to provide a clear framework for conducting reviews of decisions locally.

Delegation of other applications made under planning legislation

9.   The general powers to delegate authority contained in the
Local Government (Scotland) Act 1973 as amended[5] (the 1973 Act)
remain, but do not apply to delegating decisions on the applications relating to local development mentioned in paragraph 3. The
powers in the 1973 Act can be used to delegate decisions on planning applications relating to major development which is not
significantly contrary to the development plan[6] (though members

---

5 http://www.legislation.gov.uk/ukpga/1973/65/contents
6 Requirements for pre-determination hearings and decisions by full council
   mean planning authorities cannot delegate decisions on applications for
   planning permission for major development which is significantly contrary
   to the development plan or national developments.

may want to determine such applications), and other types of application under planning legislation, such as listed building consent, conservation area consent, hazardous substances consent and consent to display advertisements. These cases have a right of appeal to Scottish Ministers, whether they are delegated to an officer for decision or not.

Section 43A schemes of delegation

Content

10.   All planning authorities have adopted schemes of delegation as required by section 43A(1). The scheme's main role is to set out the classes of local developments which, rather than having to be determined by elected members, would be suitable for delegation to an appointed officer. The scheme itself does not have to identify who will be the appointed officer to determine applications but is to set the framework by which applications are determined by appointed officers.

11.   Section 43A(4) provides that regulations may set out the form, content and procedures for preparing and adopting a scheme of delegation. These details are set out in the Regulations.

12.   Regulation 3 specifies the content of schemes of delegation. It will largely be for planning authorities to determine which applications will be delegated to an appointed officer. Regulation 3(1) requires the scheme to describe the classes of development to which the scheme will apply and to explain with respect to every class which applications may be determined by an appointed officer. These are classes within the category of local development which authorities can identify to tailor the scheme to their own circumstances.

13.   Where an application may only be determined by an appointed officer in particular circumstances the scheme should set these out. With the removal of the statutory requirement for schemes to prevent the delegation of planning authority interest cases, local authorities can tailor their scheme of delegation to suit their circumstances and administrative procedures. The Government's view is that there should be flexibility to enable planning authorities to develop clear schemes of delegation appropriate to local circumstances.

Procedures for adoption of the scheme

14. Regulation 4 provides that where the planning authority propose to adopt a scheme of delegation under section 43A they must first send a copy of the scheme to Scottish Ministers. The planning authority are not to adopt the scheme until such time as it has been approved by Scottish Ministers. Similarly, where changes are to be made to the scheme, the planning authority must send a revised copy of the scheme they propose to adopt to Scottish Ministers for approval.

Publication of the scheme

15. Once the scheme has been approved by Scottish Ministers and adopted by the planning authority, regulation 5 requires that the planning authority make a copy of the scheme available for inspection at an office of the planning authority and in every public library in the authority's area (the legislation does not rule out electronic access to a copy). The scheme must also be published on the internet. The provisions for adoption and publication contained in the Regulations are intended to offer a straightforward process for putting schemes of delegation in place. Planning authorities remain free to take additional steps to publicise the schemes, should they consider that to be appropriate.

Use of the section 43A scheme of delegation

16. Decisions made by an appointed officer under the scheme of delegation have the same status as other decisions taken by the planning authority, other than the arrangements for reviewing the decision. Sections 43A(8) to (16) give an applicant a right to require the planning authority to review these decisions instead of a right of appeal to Scottish Ministers.

17. In cases where the planning authority receive an application for planning permission for a local development and the proposal would also require another type of consent (for example, listed building consent), there is the potential, where the former is delegated to an appointed officer for determination, for there to be two separate routes for challenging the respective decisions: one a local review and the other an appeal to Scottish Ministers. However, it will remain for the planning authority to consider which is the most effective route to determine related applications.

18.   Notwithstanding the terms of the scheme of delegation, and any restrictions it places on delegation, section 43A(6) states that the planning authority may, if they think fit, decide themselves to determine an application which would otherwise be determined by an appointed officer. Any such decision must include a statement of the reasons for which it has been taken, and a copy of the decision is to be served on the applicant.

Subsequent schemes of delegation

19.   Regulation 6 requires that the planning authority prepare a scheme of delegation at intervals of no greater than every five years. Section 43A(1)(a)(i) also prescribes that planning authorities must prepare a scheme of delegation whenever required by Scottish Ministers. The procedure for doing so will mirror that for preparing the original scheme.

Local reviews

20.   Where an application for planning permission, or for consent, agreement or approval required by a condition on such permission, is for a proposal in the category of local development falling within the scheme of delegation and has been:—

- refused by an appointed officer;
- granted subject to conditions★; or
- has not been determined within the period allowed for determination (see footnote 4),

the applicant has a right to a review of the case by the planning authority (section 43A(8)). The Regulations set out the procedures for requiring a review and the process that should then be followed.

★ Section 58(1) of the Act specifies that planning permission will expire after three years from the date on which it is granted unless the development to which it relates has been started. The Act also allows at section 58(2) that the planning authority may direct that a longer or shorter period than three years may apply. Although these time periods are not a condition to the planning permission, it is open to the applicant to seek a review against the three year time period, or any different period directed, as if it were a condition.[7] Similar provisions apply to the duration of planning permission in principle under section 59.

Notice of review

21.   Regulation 9 provides for the applicant to seek a review by giving written notice to the planning authority (the local review body). The request to review is referred to in regulation 9 as the 'notice of review'.

22.   This notice must be served on the planning authority within three months beginning with the date of the decision notice or the date of expiry of the period allowed for determining the application (see footnote 4).[8]

23.   The notice of review can be made on an e-form or its paper equivalent produced by the Scottish Government or on a planning authority form (if available). It needs to include sufficient information to allow the planning authority to review the case. Accordingly, regulation 9 sets out that the information to be provided by the applicant is:—

- the name and address of the applicant;
- the date and reference number of the application which is the subject of the review;
- the name and address of the representative of the applicant (if any) and whether any notice or correspondence required in connection with the review should be sent to the representative rather than the applicant; and
- a statement setting out the applicant's reasons for requiring the review and by what procedure (or combination of procedures), if any, the applicant wishes the review to be conducted. In this

7 The Planning etc (Scotland) Act 2006 (Consequential Amendments) Order 2009 http://www.legislation.gov.uk/ssi/2009/256/contents/made
8 For example:
(1) The date of appointed officer's decision notice is 1 September – notice of review must be received by the planning authority on or before 30 November (note: 1 December would be too late).
(2) The appointed officer has not made a decision on your planning application, and should have done so by 15 March. The last day on which you can serve the planning authority with a notice of review is 14 June.

regard the procedures that may be used are set out in regulation 13(4) and include written submissions, the holding of one or more hearing sessions and a site inspection.

24.   All matters that the applicant intends to raise in the review should be set out in or accompany the notice of review, as should all documents, material and evidence on which the applicant intends to rely.

25.   Section 43B restricts the ability of parties to introduce new matters at the review stage unless they are material to the determination of the case. This restriction does not apply to information on matters that were before the appointed officer at the time of the decision on the application or a notice of review relating to its non-determination.

26.   Regulation 9(5) makes it clear that, apart from information in the notice of review and accompanying documents, the applicant will only be able to raise matters or submit further documents to the extent permitted by the Regulations. That is either where the local review body request further written evidence or where requested as part of a hearing session. These requirements are intended to ensure that the relevant matters and items of information are provided efficiently at the start of the review process, rather than at varying points throughout the process.

27.   Regulation 18 sets out that withholding information from a notice of review which the applicant considers to be national security sensitive does not invalidate that notice. This is subject to the requirement that a written statement is included explaining that this national security consideration (as defined in regulation 18) is the reason for not submitting the information. If the local review body are unable to determine the review without the withheld information, then the case could be called in for determination by Scottish Ministers, and special procedures for dealing with national security sensitive information applied.

Local review body

28.   Regulation 7 requires that a review case is to be conducted by a committee of the planning authority comprising at least three members of the authority. The Regulations do not define an upper

limit on the number of members that should comprise the local review body: the size will be for the planning authority to determine. In cases where the local review body comprise a small
number of elected members, the authority should ensure a larger
pool of elected members is available to provide cover where appropriate.

29.　Regulation 7 requires that any meeting of the local review
body considering how the review, or stages of it, should be conducted and the review itself must be in public. Consistent with the
approach on appeals made to Scottish Ministers, the decision on
the procedure of how a case should be reviewed will be for the
local review body, although the applicant and planning authority
can indicate their preferences. While meetings are to be held in
public, this does not itself confer any entitlement on the applicant
or others to make representations, either orally or in writing. After
the initial request for review has been made, it is for the local review body to determine, in accordance with the Regulations,
whether and how any further representations or information
should be given.

30.　Membership of the local review body and administrative
arrangements for supporting the review process will be for the
planning authority to decide and so are not set out in the Regulations. Scottish Ministers expect that arrangements put in place by
planning authorities to review decisions will follow a process that
is demonstrably fair and transparent. Planning authorities should
ensure members participating in review cases receive appropriate
training in planning issues and in holding hearing sessions. In most
instances, one local review body per planning authority will carry
out the review function effectively. However, some authorities
may consider that more than one local review body would provide
an appropriate service, perhaps given the size of the geographic
area to be covered.

31.　Planning authorities will want to ensure that the local review
body are supported by appropriate administrative and legal advice
to ensure that members are guided on the review process. Where
the local review body consider it necessary to take further advice
before reaching a decision on the review it will be for the planning
authority to arrange such advice. Scottish Ministers expect that all

administrative arrangements required to support the review process should respect the principles of fairness and transparency that must underpin the operation of the system.

Notification to interested parties and publication

32.   Once a notice of review has been submitted by an applicant, regulation 10 requires the local review body to acknowledge it and make interested parties aware of the review request within 14 days of the notification. Interested parties are defined in regulation 2 and include any statutory consultees or other parties who have made, and have not withdrawn, representations in connection with the application. Regulation 10 requires statutory consultees to be notified by post of the review and for other persons either by post or by local newspaper advertisement. The Regulations allow that wherever there are notification requirements, these can include arrangements for electronic notification (see paragraph 58).

33.   The notice to interested parties must contain the following information:

- the name of the applicant and the address of the site to which the review relates;
- a description of the application;
- an explanation that copies of any representations previously made regarding the application will be considered by the local review body when determining the review;
- an indication that further representations may be made to the local review body and explain how representations may be made and by what date;
- an explanation that copies of any further representations made regarding the application will be sent to the applicant for comment;
- details of where a copy of the notice of review and other related documents can be inspected.

34.   An interested party has 14 days, beginning with the date on which this notice is given, to make representations on the review to the local review body. The local review body must send the applicant copies of all such further representations received as a result of the notice to interested parties. The applicant must be given at least 14 days to make comment to the local review body on such representations.

35.   The local review body must ensure (regulation 11) that a copy of the notice of review, and any related documents or representations are available for inspection at an office of the planning authority. The legislation does not rule out electronic access in this regard; however, it must be possible to view the information effectively. The planning authority are to give any person who requests it the opportunity to inspect and, where practicable, take copies of any review documents, until such time as the review is determined.

Compliance with development management procedures

36.   Regulation 20 sets out that where requirements set out in regulations 18-20 and 25 of the Town and Country Planning (Development Management Procedure) (Scotland) Regulations 2013[9] on notification, publication and consultation have not already been complied with by the planning authority, the local review body must ensure that these are carried out before determining the review. This is most likely to arise in instances where the review is sought on the basis of non-determination of the application (i.e. where it is not determined within the statutory timescale, or any extended period agreed upon in writing by the planning authority and applicant).

Review procedure

37.   In cases where the local review body consider that there is sufficient information from the material before it (including the notice of review, the decision notice, report on handling and any further representations from interested parties), it may under regulation 12 proceed to determine the review. It is expected that the majority of cases coming before the local review body will be accompanied by sufficient information in order for the review to be determined quickly.

9 http://www.legislation.gov.uk/ssi/2013/155/contents/made

38.   However, in some cases, it will be necessary for the local review body to obtain additional information. Part 4 and Schedule 1 to the Regulations set out the procedures for doing so. Regulation 13 confirms that the local review body may determine at any stage of the review process that further information or representations should be made to enable them to determine the review. Further information may be required by one or a combination of procedures, namely:

- written submissions;
- the holding of one or more hearing sessions;
- inspecting the land which is the subject of the review case.

39.   Under regulation 14 the local review body can hold a pre-examination meeting to consider the manner in which the review or any part of the review is to be handled. This will not be appropriate in every case. However, where, for example, there is a range of issues to be examined or more than one procedure is likely to be used to support the review process, such a meeting can clarify for the applicant and interested parties the procedures and their respective roles and help ensure the review is conducted efficiently and expeditiously. It is stressed that a pre-examination meeting will not be necessary in all but the more complex cases.

Matters which may be raised in a review

40.   Paragraphs 25 and 26, on the notice of review and accompanying documents, cover the submission of further information and the raising of new matters.

Written submissions

41.   Where the local review body requires further information to determine a review, regulation 15 allows them to request information from the applicant or any other body or person by sending a written notice. This procedure notice must set out the matters on which further information is required, specify the date when it is required by and set out who else has been asked to provide additional information (including their address details). Where the local review body issue a procedure notice requesting further information from a body or person other than the applicant, they must send a copy of that notice to the applicant.

42. When a party responds to the local review body with any further information (the procedure notice response) it must send copies to the applicant and to such other bodies or persons as the local review body specified in the procedure notice. The applicant and any other parties have a period of 14 days in which to give comments to the local review body on the procedure notice response(s), again providing copies to the applicant and other bodies or persons specified in the procedure notice.

Site inspections

43. Regulation 16 sets out the procedures for site inspections. At any point in the review process the local review body may inspect the land to which the review relates. They may do this either unaccompanied or accompanied by the applicant and any other party the local review body consider should attend. Where the inspection is to be accompanied, the local review body are required to give reasonable notice to the applicant and any interested party (defined in regulation 2). However, the local review body are not required to defer an inspection if any person to whom notice was given is not present at the appointed time.

44. The purpose of the site inspection, even if accompanied, is to allow the local review body to see the site and is not an opportunity for parties to discuss with them the merits of the case.

Hearings

45. Whenever the local review body propose to hear oral evidence, the hearing procedures apply. Schedule 1 to the Regulations contains rules for holding hearing sessions. These are intended to provide a framework within which a local review body can hear evidence from the applicant or from interested parties on specific matters only. Hearing sessions are not intended to be adversarial: the hearing should take the form of a discussion led by the local review body. Only exceptionally is it envisaged that cross-examination would be required in order to provide a thorough examination of a particular issue. The schedule provides a framework for advising the principal parties of the hearing and for them to set out clearly and in advance their respective positions.

46. Where a local review body decide that a hearing session should be held, they are to write to the parties who have an interest in the issues to be discussed at the hearing. These include:

- the applicant;
- any interested party who made representations in relation to specified matters; and
- any other body or person from whom the local review body wish to receive further representations or to provide information on specified matters.

47. The local review body must set out in writing to the above parties the matters that are intended to be considered at the hearing session – only those matters are to be considered at the hearing session. The parties then have 14 days in which to confirm their appearance at the hearing session. Whilst the applicant has an automatic right to appear at the hearing, this written confirmation entitles the other persons to appear at a hearing session.

48. The local review body will determine the arrangements for the hearing session and can vary the arrangements where it appears reasonable in the circumstances. They must give notice of these arrangements (and any change in them) to the persons entitled to appear.

49. Before a hearing session is held, those entitled to appear are expected to provide in advance a statement that fully sets out the case they intend to put forward. This is referred to in the Regulations as a hearing statement. Those entitled to appear are also required to provide a list of, and copies or extracts of, any supporting documents they intend to rely on in presenting their case. It is for the local review body to set out the timescale for submitting this information or for requesting further information from the parties following submission of their hearing statements (parties are to copy any further information they submit to the other recipients of their hearing statement). The planning authority are to make this information available to anyone requesting a reasonable opportunity to inspect it and, where practicable, take copies of it until the review is determined.

50.   The procedure to be followed at the hearing session is for the local review body to determine. The Regulations do require that before the hearing takes place, or at the outset, the local review body explain the procedure it intends to adopt, including the order both in which the specified matters are to be considered and in which parties are to be heard.

51.   The Regulations enable those entitled to appear at the hearing to do so on their own behalf or to be represented by another person. Where two or more persons have a similar interest in the issues being considered, one or more persons may appear on behalf of some or all of the parties where the local review body allow. It is not intended that the review process should be adversarial or that it must involve parties having legal or other professional representation. The intention is that the planning authority put in place a fair and transparent process that enables the local review body to reach a decision on the review.

52.   Parties entitled to appear at the hearing will be entitled to bring forward evidence from another party in support of their case. The Regulations are clear that the hearing process should take the form of a discussion led by the local review body and that cross-examination should not be permitted unless the local review body consider it necessary to ensure a thorough examination of the issues. The local review body are entitled to refuse to allow evidence to be given, and to refuse cross-examination or presentation of other issues which they consider to be irrelevant or repetitious. The local review body may from time to time adjourn the hearing session, giving such notice to the parties entitled to appear as the local review body consider reasonable in the circumstances.

Appointment of an assessor

53.   Regulation 21 permits the local review body to appoint an assessor who can advise it on specified matters. Assessors are used infrequently in the appeal system to advise on specialist or technical matters that are at issue. It is for the local review body to consider to what extent there is a role for a specialist assessor to sit with it at a particular hearing session. It is also for the local review body to decide where the assessor comes from, be it a private expert consultant, a specialist from a neighbouring authority or an expert from within the authority who has not had a previous involvement in the application. Where an assessor is appointed, those entitled to appear at the hearing session must be advised of the name of the assessor and the matters on which they are appointed to advise on. The assessor may make a written report to the local review body (and must do so if the local review body require it) after the close of the hearing session.

New evidence

54. If, having carried out any additional procedure as listed in paragraph 38, the local review body propose to take into account any new evidence which is material to the review, regulation 17 requires that it must first allow the applicant and any other relevant party (defined in regulation 17) an opportunity to make representations on that evidence.

Decision notice

55. The local review body must give a decision notice to the applicant. It is important that the terms of the decision of the local review body are clear. Under section 43A(15) the local review body have the full powers to uphold, reverse or vary a determination. Section 43A(12)(a) requires that the decision notice includes a statement of the terms in which the local review body have decided the case reviewed. The decision notice must also include a statement of the reasons on which the local review body based that decision. Regulation 22 sets out a number of requirements to ensure that there is consistency in the quality of decisions from local review bodies. The local review body must also notify every person who made (and has not subsequently withdrawn) representations in respect of the review to inform them that a decision on the review has been made, and where a copy of the decision notice is available for inspection.

56. In cases where planning permission is refused or granted subject to conditions, the decision notice must be accompanied by a notification as regards the applicant's right to take the decision to the Court of Session and their right to serve a purchase notice[10] on the planning authority. Schedule 2 to the Regulations provides the template for such notification.

Review on failure to determine the application

57.   Where the appointed officer has not determined the application within the period allowed for determination (see footnote 4), the applicant may require the planning authority to review the case. Section 43A(17) provides that if, following the applicant requiring a review on such grounds, the local review body have not conducted the review within three months, as set out in regulation 8(3), the authority shall be deemed to have refused the application. The applicant will then have the right to appeal to Scottish Ministers under section 47(1).

Electronic communication

58.   Regulation 23 sets out that, subject to certain criteria, any document required or authorised to be sent under the Regulations may be sent by electronic communications, and the requirements in the Regulations that any document is to be in writing will be fulfilled. The criteria relate to where the recipient consents, or is deemed to have agreed to receive it electronically (ie if they have already used electronic communication to send a document). The document sent by means of electronic communication must be capable of being accessed by the recipient and legible in all material respects (ie all the information must be available to the recipient to no lesser extent than it would if sent by hard copy), and must be sufficiently permanent to be used for subsequent reference.

Notification and call-in of applications

59.   Directions requiring planning authorities to notify to Scottish Ministers specified applications or classes of application where the

---

10 If planning permission is refused or granted with conditions and the owner of the land claims that the land has become incapable of reasonably beneficial use in its existing state, and cannot be so capable by the carrying out of any development which has been or would be permitted, the owner of the land may serve on the planning authority a notice requiring the purchase of the owner's interest in the land in accordance with Part 5 of the Town and Country Planning (Scotland) Act 1997.

authority is minded to grant permission, apply to applications dele-gated to an appointed officer and those before a local review body. The power to call-in applications for determination by Scottish Ministers also applies to applications before a local review body.

Transitional arrangements

60. Regulation 24(3) contains a transitional arrangement to deal with a change in the description of the hearing statement in Schedule 1. Previously this was 'an outline' of the case to be made at the hearing. This has been changed to 'fully sets out the case'. Where notice of the hearing was given prior to 30 June 2013, the previous version applies.

61. The removal of the requirement for schemes of delegation to have a restriction on delegating planning authority interest cases, will only take effect once planning authorities have adopted a new scheme with the requisite changes.

62. The change in the period for dealing with local reviews on the grounds of non-determination from two to three months (regulation 8(3)) applies to all cases. This means any such review which was applied for before 30 June 2013, where the former two month period has not elapsed before that date, moved to a three month period.

Further copies and enquiries

63. Any enquiries about the content of the Circular should be addressed to The Planning and Architecture Division, Scottish Government, 2H – South, Victoria Quay, Leith, Edinburgh, EH6 6QQ (Telephone 0131 244 7888). Copies of the circular may be obtained from the Scottish Government website at www.scotland.gov.uk/planning.

Index